MONK

From a Miniature by Samuel Cooper in the Royal Collection at Windsor

MONK

BY

JULIAN CORBETT

The Naval & Military Press Ltd

in association with

The National Army Museum, London

Published jointly by

The Naval & Military Press Ltd

Unit 10 Ridgewood Industrial Park,
Uckfield, East Sussex,
TN22 5QE England

Tel: +44 (0) 1825 749494
Fax: +44 (0) 1825 765701

www.naval-military-press.com
www.military-genealogy.com
www.militarymaproom.com

and

The National Army Museum, London

www.national-army-museum.ac.uk

CONTENTS

CHAPTER I

CHAPTER I

IN the middle of September, 1625, the great expedition
by which Charles the First and Buckingham meant to
revenge themselves upon the Spaniards for the ignominious failure of their escapade to Madrid was still
choking Plymouth harbour with disorder and confusion.
Impatient to renew the glories of Drake and Raleigh
and Essex, the young King went down in person to
hasten its departure. Great receptions were prepared
for him at the principal points of his route, and bitter was
the disappointment at Exeter that he was not to visit
the city. For the plague was raging within its walls,
and while holiday was kept everywhere else, the shadow
of death was upon the ancient capital of the west.

Hardly, however, had the King passed them by when
the citizens had a new excitement of their own. The
noise of a quarrel broke in upon the gloom of the
stricken city. Those within hearing ran to the spot and
found a sight worth seeing. For there in the light of
day, under the King's very nose, as it were, a stalwart
young gentleman of about sixteen years of age was
thrashing the under-sheriff of Devonshire within an inch

B

of his life. With some difficulty, so furious was his assault, the lad was dragged off his victim before grievous bodily harm was done, and people began to inquire what it was all about.

Every one must have known young George Monk, who lived with his grandfather, Sir George Smith, at Heavy-tree, close to Exeter. Sir George Smith of Maydford was a great Exeter magnate, and his grandson and godson George belonged to one of the best families in Devonshire, and was connected with half the rest; and had they known how the handsome boy was avenging the family honour in his own characteristic way, they would certainly have sympathised with him for the scrape he was in.

For the honour of the Monks of Potheridge in North Devon was a very serious thing. There for seventeen generations the family had lived. Ever since Henry the Third was King they had looked down from their high-perched manor-house over the lovely valley of the Tor-ridge just where the river doubles upon itself in three majestic sweeps as though it were loath to leave a spot so beautiful. By dint of judicious marriages they had managed to be still prosperous and well connected. It was no secret indeed that they claimed royal blood by two descents on the distaff side. For the grandmother of George's father, Sir Thomas, was Frances Plantagenet, daughter and co-heiress of Arthur Plantagenet, Viscount Lisle; and his grandfather's grandmother, as co-heiress of Richard Champernown of Insworth, had brought him the Cornish bordure and kinship with King John through Richard, King of the Romans, and his son, the Earl of Cornwall.

But of late things had been going very hard at Poth-

eridge. Sir Thomas had succeeded to a heavily encum-
bered estate, and his attempts at economy had done
little or nothing to better his position. An increasing
family added to his difficulties and his sorrows. Ten
children had already been born to him, and four, including
his two eldest boys, were in the grave. Thomas was now
the future heir, and then came George. After him was his
favourite brother, the quiet studious Nicholas who was
to be a parson; and then little Arthur the baby, who
became a soldier like George. George had been born on
December 8th, 1608, and was now nearly seventeen years
old. He grew up a handsome lusty boy, and from his
earliest years his daring and spirit had destined him to
be a soldier. It was the career of all younger sons of
metal, and few can have looked forward to it more
ardently than George Monk. It was the tradition of
his family. His uncle Richard had died a captain; his
uncle Arthur had fallen in 1602 at the glorious defence
of Ostend by that renowned captain, Sir Francis Vere.
His great-uncle, Captain Francis Monk, had sailed with
Drake and Norris in their famous descent upon Portugal
in 1589, and having been severely wounded at the storm
of Corunna, had died a few days afterwards when the
fleet was driven by stress of weather into Peniché.

The very soil he trod was fertile with the romance of
war. For George was born in the heart of the country
which bred the greatest of the Elizabethan heroes. The
soldiers and sailors who most adorned the great Queen's
age were living memories in his childhood, their exploits
were the tales of his nursery, their names the first words
he learnt to lisp. Hard by lived his aunt Grace, who had
married the brilliant young Bevil Grenville, heir and

grandson of the immortal Sir Richard himself. His aunt
Elizabeth was wife to Luttrell of Hartland Abbey, and
through her he could claim kinship with the Howards ;
while all around the home by Tor and Torridge were
clustered the old North Devon families with whom
Kingsley's undying romance has made us so familiar.
Nor were these influences lessened as time went on. Sir
George Smith took such a fancy to the fearless high-
spirited boy that he one day offered to educate him if
he might live half the year at Maydford. Poor em-
barrassed Sir Thomas could only consent, and George
entered a new sphere of life even fuller of romance and
adventure than the old. At Larkbere, within easy distance of his new home, lived Sir Nicholas Smith, Sir
George's eldest son, where the lad found endless cousins
to foster the dreams of Devon boyhood. But all his
games and stories there were tame beside the attractions
of his aunt Frances's house at Farringdon. For Frances
Monk had married Sir Lewis Stukeley, Vice-Admiral of
Devon, and there George must have found for a play-
fellow little Tom Rolfe, the child of Pocahontas, whose
guardian Stukeley had become since the Indian beauty's
death. Sir Lewis, too, was a cousin and intimate friend
of Raleigh himself, and George must have seen in the
company of his uncle that latest born child of the six-
teenth century and even heard his stirring adventures
from his own lips. He would certainly have missed no
opportunity of seeing the famous navigator. Raleigh
was the hero of every lad with an English spirit or an
ear for a tale. His *Discovery of Guiana* was a book
that was in every one's hands, and George and his
cousins must have known by heart its wonderful stories

of El Dorado and the Amazons. At any rate the lad
was old enough to have witnessed with eager eyes the
setting forth of Sir Walter's last expedition to find
the land of gold; to have heard with sinking heart
how his uncle Stukeley had gone forth to arrest the
hero upon his disastrous return; to mourn with all
England when Raleigh's head fell on Tower Hill, and to
burn with shame and anger when he heard the cry of
execration that rose against his uncle, the treacherous
friend who betrayed the last of the Elizabethans.

It is not difficult to imagine how a boy of George's
nature, brought up in the midst of such surroundings, must
have chafed to see his friends and kinsmen joining their
colours while he was too young to be allowed to go.
Richard Grenville, Sir Bevil's brother, whom George must
have known well, was with the expedition, and George
can have wished nothing better than to serve under him.
Sir Richard Grenville, though he afterwards disgraced
himself by his excesses in the Civil War, was then the
very hero for a boy like George. He was a typical Low
Country soldier. From an early age he had served with
Prince Maurice, the first captain of his time, in the regiment of that pattern soldier Lord Vere. In a few years
he had risen to the rank of captain, and was now commanding a company in the regiment of Sir John Borough,
chief of the staff to the expedition. It was a splendid
opportunity for George to begin his career, but it was
not to be, and it must have been with mixed feelings
that he heard the expedition was not to be delayed a
year.

When the King came down it was of course impossible
that a man of such a position as Sir Thomas Monk

should not go and pay him his respects like the other
county gentlemen.   Unfortunately there was an an-
noying difficulty in the way.   He was by this time hopelessly in debt, and so many judgments were out against
him that he was little better than a prisoner at
Potheridge.   To appear in public meant certain arrest.
There was but one escape from the dilemma, and that
was to bribe the under-sheriff.   The only question was
to whom so delicate a mission was to be entrusted, and
it cannot but raise our opinion of young George that he
was chosen for the task.   His mission was successfully
carried out, and in due course Sir Thomas rode out to
meet his sovereign with all the best blood in Devon.
But before the royal party came in sight the proceedings
were interrupted by a painful incident.   Either the
under-sheriff had blabbed, or George had been boasting
of his diplomacy.   At all events the rascally attorney
had received a bigger bribe from the other side, and now
at this solemn moment and in face of the whole county
the villain came forward and arrested Sir Thomas.

George Monk was not a boy to sit down quietly
under such an indignity.   Without saying anything to
anybody he took the first opportunity of slipping off into
Exeter regardless of the plague.   Once inside the gates
he went straight to the perfidious attorney, and having
told him in the plainest words what he thought of him,
there and then proceeded to administer the cudgelling
in the midst of which he has been already introduced,
and which was to prove his introduction to an eventful
career.

For George was in a desperate scrape.   The bruised
lawyer threatened merciless proceedings, and to cudgel an

under-sheriff was an outrage of which the law was likely to take a very serious view.   It was clear that the boy must be concealed till the storm blew over.   There was only one way of doing it.   The fleet was lying in Plymouth nearly ready to sail.   Once there he would be safe.   So George, to his intense delight we may be sure, was smuggled off and hurriedly engaged as a volunteer under his kinsman Sir Richard Grenville.   Early in October the expedition sailed.   The baffled attorney had to hang up his unserved writ on the office-files, and George Monk, by the force of the straitened circumstances of the family, found himself prematurely a soldier with the burden of an imperfect education to carry through life.

It is unnecessary to follow closely the disastrous expedition to Cadiz in 1625.   Ill-planned, ill-disciplined, ill-officered, and ill-supplied, it was doomed from the first to failure.   For young George Monk it was a bitter awakening from the dreams a boy will have of the glories of a soldier's life.   The ship in which he sailed and the company in which he served, bad as it was, can hardly have been so bad as the rest.   Grenville was at least a soldier by profession and a good officer. Borough's regiment must at least have tasted discipline. The veteran general was one of the most distinguished and scholarly soldiers of his time ; a man who had seen grow up under the Veres that immortal English brigade which by patient effort and undaunted perseverance had wrested from the Spaniards their till then unchallenged claim to be the finest infantry in the world.   He had seen more service than any man in the army, and in all questions of military science his word was law.

Thus George began his career under good masters,

and two years later he was fortunate enough to bring himself again under their command. At the head of another expedition, as ill-found as the first, Buckingham early in June, 1627, effected a landing on the Isle of Rhé, and laid siege to St. Martin, the citadel of the island. Its capture proved a more difficult matter than he had expected. Already nearly a fortnight had been expended in fruitless attempts when Buckingham's anxieties were further increased by unwelcome news. A young gentleman was announced with an important verbal message from the lips of the King. It was George Monk, who at the risk of his life had made his way through France; though ignorant of the language he had penetrated the army which lay before Rochelle, and so reached Rhé with the intelligence that a large combined naval and military force was being prepared in France to relieve the island.

For this daring service, the risks of which it is difficult to exaggerate, Sir John Borough gave him a commission as ensign in his own regiment, of which Sir Richard Grenville was major, or sergeant-major, as the rank then was, a rank involving all the duties which are now performed by adjutants, as well as the command of a company. It was most probably his kinsman's colours that the young ensign carried, and this is why he always regarded Sir Richard as his father-in-arms. For now he had begun in earnest his career as a professional soldier, and it was with every opportunity of laying the foundations of that consummate technical knowledge which afterwards distinguished him. To enforce the sound teaching of his colonel came the appalling disaster with which the expedition closed. It was a lesson he never forgot, and long after he would often grieve over the iniquitous mismanagement with which the whole affair had been conducted.

In the following year he took part with his regiment, which was now commanded by Grenville, in the last half-hearted attempt to relieve Rochelle, and then followed a period of inactivity. Buckingham was dead, and Conway with his policy of non-intervention reigned in his stead. Richelieu had no desire to retaliate ; Spain was too weak to strike a blow, and England settled down to enjoy her repose. At home there was no chance of employ-ment for the professional soldier for many years to come, and adventurous youth must look abroad.

There over the sea was a tempting prospect. Fred-erick Henry, the young Prince of Orange, had begun his brilliant career. In the previous year he had suddenly taken the offensive and snatched Grol from the very arms of the great Spinola. His treasury was overflowing with the plunder of the plate-fleet which Peter Hein had captured, and now he was besieging Bois-le-duc. Lord Vere had returned at his summons to command the English brigade and to give the young Stadtholder the benefit of his unrivalled experience. It was a name to conjure with, and volunteers flocked over from England eager for the reputation of having served under the most accomplished soldier England had yet produced. But amateur soldiering would not now satisfy George Monk, nor would his purse bear the expenses which a gentleman-private must incur. Fortunately he was not without interest, and was able to procure a commission in the regiment of which Lord Vere's kinsman, the young Earl of Oxford, had just obtained the command.

Before he could join Bois-le-duc had fallen, and it was not till 1631 that the Stadtholder took the field again. This year, however, saw the annihilation of the Spanish flotilla which attempted to surprise the island of Tholen. Lord Oxford had command of the English contingent, which was detailed to man the prince's boats, and at last George tasted the sweets of victory. The following year he was to witness one of the most brilliant campaigns which had ever been fought in the Low Countries. No sooner was the prince in motion than Venlo, Stralen, Ruremonde fell in rapid succession, and by the middle of June he had completely invested Maastricht. Three armies flew to its relief, but the prince beat them all, and at last was left to prosecute the siege unmolested. The brunt of the work in the English lines fell on Monk's regiment, but the young ensign passed through the four months of almost daily fighting without a scratch. His colonel was not so fortunate. The earl was shot dead in the second month of the siege while bringing up reinforcements to the support of the advanced picket in the trenches. On August 21st Maastricht capitulated, and the campaign was brought to a glorious conclusion. Lord Vere returned to England, having assigned the command of his regiment to George Goring, the eldest son of Lord Norwich and the future notorious cavalry officer of the Civil Wars.

It was about this time that Monk was promoted to the rank of captain, and found himself in a position which laid the foundations of his fortunes. He was in command of the colonel's company, that is to say, a double company, of which the colonel was nominal captain. For in the early days of the regimental system every colonel had his

company just as every general had his regiment; and as
the general had his lieutenant-colonel, so each colonel
had his captain-lieutenant taking precedence of all the
other captains.   It was this rank that Monk now bore,
and it was one to which great honour and responsibility
were attached.   It was in the colonel's company that the
volunteers chiefly chose to trail their pikes, and so great
was the prestige of Lord Vere's regiment, and so popular
the fascinating reprobate who commanded it, that his
company was sometimes half composed of unruly young
gentlemen who had come abroad to see the wars and sow
their wild oats.   Thus it was that Monk became personally acquainted with half the officers who afterwards distinguished themselves in the coming Civil Wars,
and not only did he make their acquaintance but he won
their respect as well.   It was only by enforcing the
strictest discipline that order could be maintained
amongst such a company.   Monk took his profession
seriously.   During his service in Holland he had made
deep study of the military sciences, no doubt in company
with old Henry Hexham, the learned and literary quarter-
master of the regiment.   He had no idea of young gentlemen playing at soldiers and disgracing the name by using
it only as an excuse for every kind of licence.   Soldiering under Captain Monk was found to be a very serious
thing.   The wildest blades were soon tamed by the im-
passive stare and rough speech of the captain-lieutenant,
young as he still was, and many there were who lived to
thank him long afterwards for the severity of the lessons
he taught.

Yet he was no mere soldier of the lecture-room and
parade-ground either, for all his science and severity.

Those who followed George Monk had to tread in thorny places, as any one who knew it not before found out at the siege of Breda. It was the last piece of service for Monk in the Low Countries, and it was the one in which he crowned his reputation for that absolute intrepidity which afterwards used to terrify the carpet-knights of the Restoration, and even make Prince Rupert hold his breath.

In 1637 Frederick found himself strong enough to invest the town with a combined army of Dutch and French, together with his English brigade. The French and English attacks were directed on an important hornwork, and here Goring's regiment had plenty of hard work and hard fighting. Monk soon found himself without a colonel; for Goring here received the wound that gave him the attractive limp the young cavaliers used afterwards so to envy, and he had to give up the active command of his regiment. But in spite of every difficulty, by the night of September 6th the English mines were almost ready. On the morrow they were to be reported complete. Monk was in command of the advanced picket in the trenches. Some attempt of the besieged to destroy the English works was only to be expected, and but for Monk's vigilance the labour of weeks might have been undone in a single night. In discharge of his duty as commander in the trenches he was making the round, and at one point he had to pass close under the hornwork. No sooner had he reached the spot than he saw a number of Spaniards dropping silently from the berme into the trenches. He had but four pikes and a couple of musketeers at his back, but without a moment's hesitation he hurled himself at the dark mass in front of him. A desperate hand-to-hand struggle ensued, till the picket, alarmed by the firing, came up, and the enemy were driven within their own works.

The mines were saved, and next morning were reported ready to be sprung. The prince at once ordered the English and French to assault, and Monk himself was told off to lead a forlorn hope of twenty musketeers and ten pikes. In support were a few sappers and two small parties like his own to right and left. After them were the whole of the gentlemen-volunteers. When all was ready the mines were discharged. A great piece of the work crumbled into ruins, and Monk, followed by his party, disappeared into the cloud of dust and smoke before it had time to settle. Without a check he reached the summit of the breach and leaped out upon a body of musketeers drawn up to resist the stormers. Completely surprised by the fury and suddenness of Monk's attack, the Spaniards broke and fled as he sprang out of the smoke. Regardless of his followers, half of whom slunk back into the breach, Monk kept on right into the enemies' work and dashed straight at a body of some six or seven score men who stood with pikes charged to receive him. But nothing would stop him now. Shouting at the top of his voice, "A Goring! a Goring!" he fell furiously on them with the handful who had followed. Fortunately the supports were close at his heels, and shaken by his desperate onslaught, the Spaniards broke before the charge of the volunteers. In disorder they fled into an interior work followed by the English and French, who rushed bravely to the rescue, and the hornwork was won.[1]

---

[1] *A True and Brief Relation of the famous Siege of Breda*, etc., by Henry Hexham. Delft, 1637.

It was the beginning of the end. The loss of the hornwork made the city untenable, and a few weeks later the garrison surrendered. It was Monk's last stroke in the service of the States-General. In the following year, as he lay in winter-quarters at Dort, the burghers took deep offence at some disturbances of which his young reprobates had been guilty, and claimed to try them for the offence. No one had a higher sense of his duty to his employers than Monk, and no one stood up more stoutly for the rights of the men under his command. He insisted on settling the matter by court-martial. The burghers appealed to the States. Such cases were not unknown, and had always been decided in favour of the military. But Dort was an important town, and not to be offended lightly. The States-General decided in favour of the burgomaster, and the prince had to order Monk and his troops into quarters which were by no means a change for the better. Monk was highly offended. He considered the honour of the army was outraged in his person. Unable to support the indignity, and disgusted at the want of consideration shown to a man of his services, he resigned his commission, and resolved to place his sword and experience at the service of his own country.

CHAPTER II

THE great drama was about to begin. The star-chamber
had given judgment in Hampden's case: the prayer-
book had been read in Edinburgh; and it was amidst
ominous mutterings of coming evil that Captain Monk
set foot once more upon his native shore.

How great a tragedy was to develope itself out of
the prologue upon which the curtain was about to rise,
no one as yet could tell. Still less were there any to
guess that the plain Low Country officer stepping on to
the Dover beach was the man who was to cut the knot
of the last act and end the play in a blaze of triumph.

We can see him clearly as he rides towards London,
brooding, as his manner was, on the ungrateful treatment he had received at the hands of his masters. He
is now in his thirtieth year, rather short than tall, but
thickset and in full possession of the physical strength
which the ill-starred under-sheriff had tasted at Exeter
years ago; and as with an air of dogged self-reliance he
sits erect upon his horse, handsome, fresh-coloured, well-
knit, he looks every inch a soldier. Quietly chewing his
tobacco for company, as the fashion was, he speaks little
to those who overtake him on the road, except perhaps

it is to grumble at the Mynheers when the subject turns
that way.   He answers strangers with a blunt, almost
rude brevity, at which men are offended, but which
somehow they feel little inclined to openly resent.   He
is an ill-mannered, thick-headed soldier, they say, and it is
best to leave him alone to take his own way.

And indeed he was little more.   He was frankly the
ideal of a soldier of fortune, versed in his art to the
point of pedantry, wary to the verge of craftiness,
fearless to a fault, jealous of his honour as the knight
of La Mancha himself.   The name by which such men
were known is unfortunate, for it has led to much
misconception of their character.   Then it was well
understood to mean a soldier by profession, no more nor
less than what every officer in our army is to-day.   The
ideal soldier of fortune was marked not so much by his
readiness to change his colours as by his blind devotion
to those with which for the time being he was engaged.
Until the period of his commission, or of the war or
campaign for which he had engaged was ended, his
loyalty to his paymasters was as ungrudging as it was
unassailable.   Nothing would have induced him to
enter a service which he considered dishonourable,
but having once engaged he fought and toiled and
bled in contemptuous indifference to the political manœuvres of the men whose commission he held.   To look
upon such men as cruel, unprincipled adventurers is the
very reverse of the truth where worthy pupils of the
heroic Veres are concerned.   We must remember that
it was in their school that Monk learnt his trade, and
not in that which produced men like the Turners and
Dalziells and brought disgrace upon the name of the

soldier of fortune. They were men who could only teach
virtues, though perhaps the only virtues they could teach
were honesty and obedience. At any rate that was the
lesson which Monk learnt. To be true to his paymaster,
that was his rule in life; to obey the civil authority
which employed him, that was his political creed. Such
was the code which Monk brought home with him from
the Low Countries. Simple and rude as it was, it was
all he had to guide him through the labyrinth he was
about to tread.

As yet the Revolution stirred but in restless slumber,
and it is probable that it was not the prospect of civil
strife which brought Monk to England in search of
employment. Prince Rupert and his brother were at
Court in hopes of getting their uncle's aid for the re-
covery of the Palatinate; and the King, sobered by failure,
was turning and doubling every way to shirk the responsibility and enjoy the credit of assisting his beautiful
and unfortunate sister. Of all the schemes which were
suggested to this end the most extraordinary was the
project for the colonisation of Madagascar. The idea
was that a thousand gentlemen should join, each with
a thousand pounds and a number of servants. The King
was to provide twelve ships from the navy, and thirty
merchantmen were to complete the fleet. Every
adventurer was to sail in person, and the whole was to
be commanded by Prince Rupert himself, with the title
of Governor-General of Madagascar or St. Lawrence.
But Elizabeth grew anxious about her son, and opposed
the wild scheme in which she could see no reason.
"As for Rupert's romance," she wrote to Roe, "about
Madagascar, it sounds more like one of Don Quixote's

conquests when he promised his trusty squire to make
him king of an island." In the end practical merchants
and seamen threw so much cold water on the scheme
that it began to lose favour, and Rupert did not go.

Meanwhile all the world was run mad on the romantic
adventure. Davenant wrote a little epic about it, which
made Endymion Porter exclaim, himself as mad as the
rest :

> "What lofty fancy was't possest your braine,
>   And caus'd you soare into so high a straine ?"

Suckling so far forgot himself in the craze of the hour
as to write a copy of verses that may still be read without a blush. Even the phlegmatic Captain Monk was
carried away. Man of the new time as he was, in the
bottom of his heart he was Elizabethan. The project
was more than enough to revive the dreams of his
Devonshire boyhood, of Raleigh, of Guiana, and the early
days of Virginia, and he promised to go. But it was
not to be. Ere long he withdrew, either because his
native shrewdness showed him it was all a bubble or
else because the curtain was up at last, and he turned
to the thrilling play beside which the Madagascar adventure was only a childish fairy tale.

Scotland was to be coerced into conformity, and in
the bustle of preparation Monk saw his chance. To
every soldier in England his name must have been
perfectly familiar. Every young gentleman who had
seen any service was hurrying to the King's standard
on the chance of a commission, and the majority of
them would be only too glad to claim George Monk
as their father-in-arms, and boast of their service in the

colonel's company of the crack regiment in the Low
Country Brigade.

Nor did Monk lack powerful friends.   He was a wide-
kinned man, so wide that it is impossible to trace the
multitudinous ramifications of his family.   He had con-
nections in high places, and they began to take him up.
Above all Lord Leicester seems to have found a pleasure
in pushing his distinguished young kinsman's fortunes,
and at this moment there was no better friend a young
man could have than Robert Sidney, second Earl of
Leicester.   His family was just now rising into high
favour.   His brother-in-law, the Earl of Northumberland,
was Lord Admiral, while for sister-in-law he could claim
the lovely Countess of Carlisle herself.

This "Erinnys of the North," as Warburton called
her, for whom Waller could forget awhile his Sacharissa,
who made Davenant sing his sweetest, and wrung from
Suckling his most lascivious note, was still the reigning
beauty of the Court.   As she entered middle age her
charms seemed only to ripen.   Her eyes were as bright,
her wit as keen, her vivacity as sparkling as ever.   The
only change was in the field of her conquests.   Weary
of breaking the hearts of fops and poets, she was seeking
new excitement in political intrigue and new pleasures
in charming tried leaders of men such as Pym and
Strafford.   At this moment a blunt manly soldier like
Captain Monk was just the man to find favour in her
capricious eyes.   Monk was always soft-hearted with
a woman, and his admiration of such a beauty must have
been frank and undisguised.   Whatever was the cause,
he found her willing to support Lord Leicester's request
for his advancement.   The task was not difficult.

Officers of tried worth who could be trusted in the
quarrel were in high demand for lieutenant-colonels of
the newly-raised regiments. Half the colonels were
noblemen of little experience, and the rest were occupied
with their duties on the staff. Monk, as a man who
despised politics and was without convictions, was in
every way fitted for a command, and his fair friend was
soon able to hand him his commission as lieutenant-
colonel of Lord Newport's regiment of foot.

Monk soon found plenty of work to do; but all his
efforts to turn his men into soldiers were thrown away.
In June, 1639, to his intense disgust a pacification was
patched up with the Scots, and the First Bishops' War
came to an ignominious end before a blow had been struck.
To Monk, whose narrow but enthusiastic patriotism had
been only increased by his service abroad, such a fiasco was
deeply mortifying. With a stupid constancy, for which
it is impossible not to love him, he clung through life
to the fixed idea that one Englishman was any day worth
two or three of any other nation. To face an army of
Scots for months and then come to terms without fighting
was a piece of pusillanimity he could not understand, and
never forgot.

Nor did the conduct of the Second Bishops' War
mend his opinion of the King. His regiment was amongst
the first that were ready to take the field. It was
present at the rout at Newburn Ford, where its lieutenant-colonel distinguished himself by saving the
English guns. But with that disgraceful action the
campaign ended. Monk and a few other officers at the
Council of War urged every argument which the pedantic
strategy of the day could suggest in order to induce the

King to attack the Scots with the concentrated army which was now strengthened with the Yorkshire and Durham trained-bands. But all was in vain, and an armistice preliminary to peace was concluded at Ripon, by which the two northern counties were left in possession of the Scots as security for a war-indemnity.

For these two miserable failures Monk never forgave the King. To the end of his life he used to harp on the fatal mistake Charles made in not following the advice he gave, and to the last maintained, with characteristic ignorance of the real questions at issue, that all the blood which flowed in the following years was to be imputed to the folly of sparing it then.

While the Scots were eating up the fat of the land and Monk was fretting at the part he had to play, the plot was thickening fast. The Long Parliament had met and Strafford was brought to bay. The breach between King and Parliament was widening daily, and Charles was foolish enough to listen to schemes which the most hairbrained of his courtiers devised for dragging the army into the quarrel. Men ready to coerce the Houses were to be placed in command, and the army was to be brought up to London and the Tower snatched from the hands of Lord Newport, who was now constable. But there was a difficulty in the way. The Low Country officers, true to their principles, refused to have anything to do with the plot, and the conspirators fell out before the question of command could be settled. Goring, who had been promised the post of Lieutenant-General, in a fit of spite betrayed the plot to Lord Newport. Newport told Pym, and at the critical moment when Strafford's fate hung in the balance Pym played the information as a trump-card.

The effect was electrical, and its sequel of no little consequence to Monk. The revelation produced a revulsion of feeling which brought Strafford's head to the block, and Lord Leicester, as a favourite with both King and Parliament, was hastily summoned from Paris to succeed him as Lord Lieutenant and Commander-in-Chief in Ireland.

As the truth about the army-plots was allowed to transpire the worst was believed of the King's intentions. The belief even began to spread that Charles was privy to a popish plot, of which the queen was the centre, to bring troops from Ireland for the utter subversion of the Protestant faith. Then into the midst of the growing distrust there burst like a thunderbolt the news of the Irish rebellion, and the smouldering fires of the Reformation, which had slumbered since the great days when they scorched the throne of Spain, burst into a flame. On the heels of the news came down a letter from Scotland in which the King commended to Parliament the care of reducing the rebels to obedience. The Commons voted on the spot an army of eight thousand men and confidently called for volunteers. But that was not all. The weapon was easy to forge, but it must now be placed out of the King's reach. It was not enough that Leicester was made Captain-General. His second in command must also be a man in whose honour and fidelity the House had implicit confidence.

Astley and Conyers were unwilling to serve. It says not a little for the reputation which Monk had won both as a man and a soldier, that his name was the next mentioned.[1] It was proposed that he should be given the command as Lieutenant-General, with Henry

[1] Captain Fox to Pennington, *S. P. Dom.* November 11th, 1641.

Warren, his veteran major and devoted friend, as his
Adjutant-General, or Sergeant-major-general, as it was
then called.   It was a splendid chance, but Monk was
doomed to disappointment.   The Houses were suddenly
informed that Ormonde had been chosen for the command and commissioned Lieutenant-General by the King,
and the tactics of the Parliament had to be changed.
It was determined to raise an army by an Impressment
Bill, to which a clause was to be added vesting the control of it in their own hands.   As the month of November wore on and it was still in debate, by every post
came news of fresh atrocities committed by the Papist
rebels upon the English Protestants.   Never perhaps
again till the story of the Cawnpore massacre set the
nation's teeth, did such a frenzy of revenge take possession of the people.   More and more troops were voted
every week.   Every tale, no matter how hideous or im-
probable, was greedily believed.   It was necessary that
something should be done at once.   Leicester was ordered
to raise two regiments of foot and one of horse by volun-
tary enlistment, and that the Parliament might keep a
firm hand on the reins it was further resolved that he
should submit the list of officers he proposed to commission to the Houses for approval.   Monk was named for
lieutenant-colonel and Warren for major of Leicester's
own regiment of foot.   Both were at once approved; and
the nominations of Leicester's two sons, Lord Lisle and
Algernon Sidney, as well as that of Sir Richard Grenville, were confirmed for the horse.

On February 21st, 1642, Colonel Monk landed in
Dublin at the head of the Lord-General's regiment of
foot.   It was a splendid body of men, two thousand

strong and officered by the flower of the disbanded army
of the north. And with him was Sir Richard Grenville,
commanding four hundred of Leicester's new regiment of
horse. Over the scenes which followed there is no need
to linger. In fire and blood the wretched Irish had to
do penance for the outburst of savagery to which they
had been goaded by Strafford's imperious rule. The most
important operation of the campaign of 1642 was the
expedition for the relief of the English settlements in
Kildare and Queen's County. With two thousand five
hundred foot under Monk, five hundred horse under
Lucas, Coote, and Grenville, and six guns, Ormonde
left Dublin on April 2nd, and by the 9th had successfully relieved Athy, Maryborough, and some smaller
settlements. The work was accomplished with all the
horrible accompaniments which characterised Irish warfare. "In our march thither," wrote an officer in
Monk's regiment, " we fired above two hundred villages.
The horse that marched on our flanks fired all within
five or six miles of the body of the army; and those
places that we marched through, they that had the rear
of the army always burned. Hitherto we met not with
any enemy to oppose, yet not a mile nor a place that we
marched by, that the dead bodies of the rebels did not
witness our passage." But the most difficult part of the
enterprise yet remained. Some thirty miles beyond the
river Nore, in a country swarming with rebels, lay several
garrisons yet unrelieved. Ormonde's provisions were
running so short that to reach them by a regular operation was impossible; but sooner than abandon them
Grenville, Lucas, and Coote undertook to make a dash
to their aid with the cavalry, while Monk covered the

retreat. On the morning of Saturday the 10th, in the dead of night, the horse sallied from Maryborough, and succeeded in passing the river unobserved. The Irish at once took the alarm, and seized the only two fords by which they could return. That at Portnahinch they barred by an intrenchment, and leaving the other open they laid a strong ambush along the dangerous causeway by which it was approached. There, certain of their prey, they quietly waited to wreak a terrible vengeance on Grenville's ruthless troopers. On Monk rested the only chance of escape. Early on Monday morning, with a party of six hundred musketeers, he attacked a neighbouring castle, which belonged to one of the rebel leaders, hoping to draw to its relief the forces which held the fords; but not a man would they stir. In desperation he determined to force the pass at Portnahinch, but on reaching it he found the river so swollen that it was impassable for foot. The last hope seemed gone, but Monk was not to be beaten. Seizing every point of vantage on his own bank, he placed his musketeers with such skill that the Irish could neither abandon nor reinforce their intrench-ments. Assured that the horse must mean to force a passage at this point under cover of Monk's fire, they at last withdrew the whole of their strength from the other ford, and while Monk occupied them with a deadly fusilade, Grenville and his exhausted comrades rode unmolested along the abandoned causeway and reached Maryborough in safety.[1]

---

[1] The above details are from a letter amongst the Longleat MSS., written by one of Monk's captains to a correspondent in England, a transcript of which was most kindly sent me by the Marquis of Bath.

The horse were saved, and, now his object was accomplished, Ormonde began to retire to Dublin. It was in the course of this march that he won his brilliant action at Kilrush. Monk was present with the staff during the general's reconnaissance on the eve of the battle, and we may credit him with at least a share of the masterly tactics by which the victory was obtained. That Ormonde appreciated his services is certain, for on this occasion he was mentioned in despatches "for the alacrity and undaunted resolution" he had displayed.

By the end of June eight more regiments, including Lord Lisle's carbineers, were landed in Dublin, and the Parliament seemed to have exhausted all the resources it could spare for Ireland. The Civil War was beginning. By straining every nerve it could only hold its own against the King in England, and the Irish army was left to shift for itself. Constant forays became a necessity, and indeed were the only operations possible. In these no one was so successful as Monk. He displayed in them all the qualities which endear a commander to his men, and soon no officer in the army was so popular with rank and file as he. No one, they used to say, was too sick or sorry for action, and nobody's boots were too bad for a march, when the word was passed that "honest George" was off foraying again. It became a joke that his regiment was the purveyor for the whole of Dublin.

This was hardly the work that Monk had promised himself when he volunteered for Ireland; but at any rate it was a great relief to him that he was leaving behind the politics which he detested and only half understood for some hard fighting which was his meat and drink. But he was to be sadly disappointed. Lord

Leicester, commissioned by the King and paid by the
Parliament, was still in England, detained by orders from
Oxford. In Ormonde Charles knew he had a representative in every way satisfactory. He was a royalist
above suspicion. The advent of Leicester could only
strengthen the hands of the Lords Justices, who represented the Lord Lieutenant in his absence. These men
were staunch Parliamentarians, and made it their business to oppose Ormonde's influence in every way. Indeed
their enemies accused them of deliberately thwarting his
operations in order that, by allowing the rebellion to
spread, there might be a larger area of land for confiscation. In return for providing money for the suppres-
sion of the rebellion an influential body of London
capitalists had obtained from Parliament a concession of
one quarter of the land which should become liable to
confiscation ; and it is to be feared the Lords Justices
were to some extent interested in this gigantic job. The
Lords Justices had their fortunes to make, and they saw
them in their power of distributing the forfeited lands.
Their interests as well as their opinions were in sympathy with the parliamentary cause. Thus Ormonde
represented for them a double danger, and without ac-
cusing them of actually fostering rebellion, it is certain
that they did their best to discredit Ormonde with the
King in order to procure his recall.

To seek Monk's attitude in the strife we need not go
far. If he had any sympathies either way, which is very
doubtful, they were certainly at this time parliamentarian.
Indeed a slight he received about this time must
have sharply spurred him to the side to which contempt
for the King, anxiety about his pay, and the influence of

his friends the Sidneys already inclined him. In May Sir Charles Coote, the governor of Dublin, had been killed in action. No one deserved to succeed him so well as "honest George." No one had done so much for the place, above all, in keeping in temper the troops who were always on the verge of mutiny for want of pay and clothes and food. Accordingly Lord Leicester, on the recommendation of the Lords Justices, sent over a commission by which he was appointed governor at a double salary of forty shillings a day, a little addition which made the post doubly dear to the soldier of fortune; but hardly had the commission arrived when there came a letter direct from the King approving the permanent appointment of Lord Lambert, who had been acting as Coote's deputy, and Monk found the governorship and his forty shillings a day snatched out of his very mouth.

Important as this affair was to poor Monk, it was but one of many such passages between the two parties. Ormonde, on the whole, was getting the upper hand; but the condition of friction which this state of things set up could have but one result. The rebels gained ground by strides. In September General Preston landed from Spain with quantities of supplies of all kinds for their use. A popish plot was winded once more. A new design was suspected of raising an army for the King in Ireland with Catholic money and arms. Ormonde's popularity was growing alarming. What was to prevent him suddenly joining hands with the rebels and turning with the whole army upon the Parliament? How could it then withstand the King? An old prophecy was in every one's mouth:

> " He that would old England win
> First with Ireland must begin."

The action which the Commons took at this crisis gives us a startling peep beneath the boards where the wire-pullers sat. Joint-committees were sent out to the various provinces, consisting each of two delegates, one nominated by the Commons and one by the Syndicate which was working the Irish concession. Reynolds and Goodwin were the two appointed for Dublin. On their arrival they were at once, without a shadow of right, admitted to the Council, and set to work to put Lisle at the head of the army instead of Ormonde, and oust from the governorship of Dublin the man who had supplanted the parliamentary candidate. They even tried to commit the army to an oath of fealty to Parliament, but £20,000 was all the money they had brought to satisfy arrears, and it was not enough to allay the distrust of the soldiers.

As the winter advanced the distress and discontent of the troops increased. Their clothes were in rags, many had not even boots to their feet, and proper food could hardly be obtained. They cried aloud for their pay, and the delegates saw a new device must be tried to silence the dangerous clamour. In testimony of the goodwill of the Parliament, they offered all such as should be willing to accept it a grant of rebel land in satisfaction of arrears. The idea was extremely ingenious and nearly succeeded. Monk was far too dull a man to see through it, and he at once subscribed the agreement. But there were many to point out what it meant. It was soon seen to be a mere device to commit the army to the cause of the Parliament, and those who had so hastily

signed insisted on withdrawing, for ruin stared them in
the face. Ormonde had received instructions from the
King to negotiate a pacification with the Irish rebels.
In him the army saw their only chance of redress, and in
spite of all the delegates could do they set out their
grievances in a loyal address and sent it to the King.

By the end of January, 1643, Ormonde, strengthened
by a new commission from Oxford, was able to exclude
Reynolds and Goodwin from the Council, and after a
few weeks spent in undisguised attempts to suborn the
troops, they sailed for England, just in time to escape
arrest on the royal warrant.

The cavalier had triumphed; but until he had
carried out his instructions to come to terms with the
rebels his victory was useless to the royal cause. The
negotiations went on but slowly. The Anglo-Irish lords
of the Pale were anxious for peace, but the Lords
Justices were careful to obstruct Ormonde's diplomacy
by forcing him into military operations. Their policy
deferred the cessation, but only to make it more inevitable. Each expedition left the Government more
exhausted. The scanty resources that remained were
only the more rapidly consumed, and, though with the
singleness of purpose that had marked his conduct
throughout, Monk strained every nerve to do his duty,
no real impression was made upon the rebels.

Very shortly after Ormonde's victory at Ross, Preston
was threatening Ballinakill, twenty miles north of Kil-
kenny, and the garrison was only saved for the time
by Monk dashing out of Dublin with half a regiment
and four troops. Close to the town he met a large
number of rebels, put them to flight, relieved the garrison,

and returned safe to Dublin. Still food grew scarcer.
Preston knew his game was a waiting one, and avoided
an engagement. As time went on the English army
could hardly be kept together. The troops were scattered
about, working on lands by which the chief officers were
pacified. Desertions in all ranks took place wholesale.
Negotiations for peace were revived, and the military
situation was in complete stagnation.

It was about this time that Monk heard of his father's
death, and probably in consequence of this he asked and
obtained leave from Ormonde to go home. There was an
annuity of £100 a year to look after, which was left
him by Sir Thomas's will, but the matter had to wait.
In June Preston and O'Neill, the leader of the native
Irish party, had advanced almost within touch of each
other into King's County and West Meath. Ormonde,
hoping to bring them to their knees, determined once
more to try and force them to an action. A strong force
of two thousand foot and three hundred and fifty horse
was prepared and Monk called on to take the command.
On the strength of his leave he refused, and all the
pressure which the Lords Justices could bring to bear
on him was of no avail. Sir John Temple, the father
of Sir William, was the man who at last induced him to
consent, and he marched. Under the nose of Preston, with
less than a third of his numbers, he succeeded in relieving
the important garrison of Castle-Jordan, but want of
provisions rendered a forward movement impossible, and
he was compelled to retreat without coming to an
engagement.

On all sides the rebels were closing in. Ormonde learnt
that Lord Inchiquin in Munster was in as desperate a

position as himself. Still he would not grant the rebels
their terms, and Monk, in spite of all his grievances, stood
by him with obstinate devotion. No more was heard
of his leave, and all through those terrible weeks of
danger and privation he held on to encourage the troops
with his presence. In the autumn he was operating
successfully in Wicklow, and occupying positions there
to hold Lord Castlehaven and General Preston in check
till the harvest was secured. But from the north O'Neill
was advancing, and Monk was recalled to reinforce Lord
Moore, who was opposing the Ulster Nationalists. Once
more every effort was paralysed by the commissariat.
Moore was killed, and Monk had to retire to Dublin to
find all he had gained in Wicklow was lost.

Further resistance was hopeless. The army was at
starvation point. Preston was raiding within two miles
of Dublin gates, and north and south O'Neill and Castlehaven held in irresistible force the whole of the country
on which the English relied for supplies. To add to
Ormonde's embarrassments, ever since the Scots had
declared for the Parliament Charles had been pressing
him to conclude an armistice with the rebels upon any
terms, and at last he gave way. On September 15th
was signed that cessation from which, in insane contempt for the deepest feelings of his people, the King
hoped so much, and which was at last to bring upon him
so terrible a retribution.

CHAPTER III

As early as April Ormonde had received secret instructions which can have left him in no doubt as to the real meaning of the King's anxiety for the success of the negotiations. No sooner was the matter settled than the Lieutenant-General busied himself in carrying out his master's orders. Every man that could be spared was to be sent to the assistance of the King against the Scots, and the greatest care was to be exercised that they sailed under commanders who could be trusted.

Meanwhile, in face of the catastrophe they had so long apprehended, the parliamentary agents were not idle. They promised the troops full discharge of arrears and every other inducement to enter their service, and with such success that Ormonde considered it necessary to take the precaution of demanding the signature of a "protestation" from the officers who were to go to England. To his intense disgust Monk was called upon to formally pledge himself to be true to the flag under which he was about to serve. That he had any serious objection to the royal cause is hardly probable. His friends, Lord Lisle and Algernon Sidney, were not in Dublin to influence him. Monk, with the rest of the

D

officers, must have long lost faith in parliamentary
promises of pay ; and, moreover, through the Commons'
antipathy to martial law, there had been trouble in Ireland
of the same nature as that which led to his leaving the
Dutch service. Then the prospect of coming to blows
with the Scots, before whom he had been disgraced, had
irresistible attractions for him. Morally there was nothing
to prevent him entering the royal service. Although paid
by the Parliament it was the King's commission he held.
But to be asked to pledge himself to the politics of those
for whom he fought was in his eyes a monstrous proposal, while to be called on to swear fidelity to the man
whose commission he held was an insult. Rigid even
to pedantry in his notions of military honour, he did
not know what it was to swerve a hair's-breadth from
the duty of his place. Through jealousy and disappointment, through every danger and temptation, he had
been true to Ormonde, and now his reward was to be
suspected of being able to forget what was due to himself as a soldier. It was more than he could tamely
endure. Ormonde presented the protestation, and Monk
flatly refused either to sign or swear, nor did he scruple
to say plainly what he thought of it. Only one man
had the spirit or honesty to follow his example, and
that was Colonel Lawrence Crawford, the sturdy Scot
whose bigotry would not now permit him to draw sword
against the Covenant, and was ere long to bring down
upon him the merciless resentment of Cromwell.

Monk was deprived of his regiment, and Warren
reluctantly accepted the command. Ormonde could do
no less, but so great was his respect for Monk's character
and capacity that he took no further step. Monk was

simply granted leave to go home, and there the matter might have rested but for the injudicious conduct of his sanguine young admirer, Lord Lisle. The Parliament was about to send reinforcements into Ulster, and the choice of a commander lay between the Scotchman Munroe and Lisle. Munroe's recommendation was his influence with the old Scotch colonists, while Lisle claimed that he could command the services of Monk, and through him half Ormonde's army. Lord Digby, the King's Secretary of State, although his good opinion of Monk was unshaken by the rumours he heard, still took the precaution of warning Ormonde, and writing in the King's name a very flattering letter to the colonel himself. So far all was well. His spotless integrity was enough to lift him above every suspicion. Ormonde seems still to have had enough confidence in him to allow him to sail with the troops to Chester, when somehow he got to know that a special messenger from Pym himself had arrived in Dublin to urge Monk to prevent the troops joining the King.

It now was impossible for Ormonde to ignore the danger of the injured colonel's power for evil so long as he remained with the army, and he felt it his duty to send him to Bristol under arrest. Instructions went with him that he should be confined till further orders from Oxford, whither the Lieutenant-General sent a report of the step he had taken. "In the meantime," he says in his letter to Sir Francis Hawley, the governor of Bristol, "I must assure you that Colonel Monk is a person very well deserved of this kingdom, and that there is no unworthy thing laid to his charge, therefore I desire you to use him with all possible civility."

Hawley, who was one of Monk's innumerable kinsmen, interpreted his instructions so widely as to release the colonel on parole at once, indignant, as it seems, that a man of such distinguished service should be treated so shabbily. But his responsibility was not to last long. Digby showed Ormonde's despatch to the King, who decided at once that Monk was a man worth the trial to gain, and he was sent for to Oxford.

Lord Digby had ready for the injured soldier a most flattering reception. "Honest George" was but a child in the hands of such a man. The brilliant Secretary of State was irresistible with his polished wit, his scholarly discourse, and great personal charm. It was he who had provided Charles with his most trusted counsellors. It was he who had beguiled Sir John Hotham into betraying his trust at Hull. He had even a personal experience of ratting himself, and easily persuaded the colonel to give him his company to Christchurch, where the King lodged.

The inevitable result ensued. No one had in a greater degree the trick of attaching such men to him than Charles. No one had a keener eye for a weakness to be played upon. He was taking the air in the gardens of the College when the two visitors arrived, and we can see them even now as they meet amidst the trim lawns. The artful secretary making his presentation in a few flattering words that say everything to the King: the stalwart soldier saluting somewhat abruptly with a frank honest stare; and Charles with his careworn smile saying something that brings a flush to the handsome face he scrutinises. We can hear him speak of the daring journey to Rhé, of the breach at Breda, of the guns at Newburn, and of all that has since been done in Ireland. He is glad also to have so great an authority on military science in Oxford, as he wants some confidential advice on the prosecution of the war. We can see the look of half-amused surprise as honest George "deals very frankly with his Majesty," and tells him his army is only a rabble of gentility, whose courage and high birth are worthless beside the growing discipline that Fairfax and Skippon and Cromwell are teaching his enemies. Let the King cut down his numbers to ten thousand men, properly organised and equipped; let him officer them with real Low Country soldiers, and send the high-born amateurs to the right-about, and with such an army he would bring the rebels to their knees in a trice. It is hardly, perhaps, the answer his Majesty expected, but he trusts to hear more of the matter another time. So Monk is dismissed, delighted at the King's good sense and condescension. Pay, arrears, and all are forgotten. He is taken by assault, and soon informs Lord Digby he is ready to take service in the royal army.

The only question now was where the man who was worth a trial to gain should be employed. There was a general impression that he should go to Devonshire, where his eldest brother, Sir Thomas, was doing good work. But Monk made difficulties. A civil war in his native county was peculiarly distasteful to a man of his nature. Besides, his heart was not there. He had left it with the regiment that was devoted to him, and that was now, with the rest of the Irish brigade, investing Nantwich under Lord Byron. The fall of the place was looked on as certain; when all at once in the midst of the Christmas revels there was a cry that help was at hand. Under peremptory orders from London, Fairfax had left his winter quarters about Lincoln, and had succeeded in penetrating Cheshire with a large force by the end of January. There was no doubt about Monk's destination then. The hardships of the unexpectedly long siege and two small reverses had seriously affected the temper of the Irish brigade, and their idol was hurried to infuse a better spirit into his old comrades for the coming struggle.

The sight of "honest George" was as good as another regiment to the besiegers, and when he took his place, pike in hand, at the head of the first file of his old corps, Lord Byron saw his force had got a new heart. Monk had in his pocket a commission to raise a regiment and a promise of the post of Major-General to the brigade, but in spite of this and of Warren's entreaties to take his old command, he insisted on retaining his humble position.

The very day after Monk joined the alarm was given that Fairfax was at hand, and the position of the Royalists was suddenly found to be desperately weak. Byron's army was investing the town on both sides of the river Weaver. Warren's and four other regiments of foot were on the left bank, and it was on this side that Fairfax was advancing. On the first news of his approach they had taken up a position at Acton Church, about a mile in rear of their works, where they intended to stop his advance, while to prevent a sortie of the garrison a small guard was left to hold the bridge by which the town was reached. On the other side of the river was Lord Byron with the rest of the infantry and all the

horse. Communications had been kept up hitherto by
fords, but a sudden thaw had so swollen the river as to
render them impracticable. Only by a ride of six miles
could the horse reach the foot at Acton, and the way lay
through lanes that the melting snow had rendered almost
impassable. Still there was but one thing to do, and
Byron galloped off along the river through the slush and
mire, trusting there might yet be time to get round
before the enemy attacked.

Meanwhile Fairfax had come in sight of the isolated
foot. Monk's old Low Country comrade saw his advantage immediately, and continued his advance with the
intention of cutting his way through the infantry to join
hands with the garrison before Byron could come to the
rescue. Nearer and nearer he pressed, opening a way
through the hedges as he came straight across country.
Suddenly there was an alarm in the rear-guard. In
spite of the mud and narrow lanes and swollen river
Byron was upon him at last. Quick as thought "Form
your files to the rear and charge for horse!" was the
order which rang from Fairfax's lips, and Byron's breath-
less troopers were hurled back from a solid wall of pikes
and muskets. Three of the Parliament regiments had
reversed their front and with the rest Fairfax dashed at
Monk and his friends. Warren's was in the centre,
and it broke at once. The rest stood firm but with
flanks exposed. Pike in hand Monk raged through his
disgraced regiment and rallied it for one more charge.
Again it broke, and Fairfax poured in between the wings
a resistless flood. At the same moment the garrison
sallied out, forced the guard at the bridge, and fell upon
the Royalist rear. All was over. Drowned in a sea of

armed men that flowed on every side of them, the regiments which till now had held their ground could resist no longer. Surrender or flight was all that was left. Too late Monk found the regiment he was so proud of would not fight in such a cause. He even had to hear it said that a number of his men had turned their fire on the hard-pressed wings. Acton Church, around which the train was parked, was hard by, and thither with the rest of the officers he took refuge. For a while Byron hovered round to try a rescue with the horse, but the attempt was hopeless. Church, guns, baggage and all were surrendered, and after barely a week's service in the King's army Monk found himself a prisoner.

A few days afterwards nearly the whole of his old regiment had enlisted with Fairfax, while he and Warren were sent prisoners to Hull. But for such a man Hull was not safe enough. It had but recently been relieved, and was not out of danger so long as Lord Newcastle was at York. Fairfax and the other officers who had fought by Monk's side in the Low Countries knew well the value of his services, and impressed upon the Parliament that he was "a man worth the making," and not without effect. He was ordered up to London with Warren, and on July 8th brought to the bar of the House. There the two unfortunate officers were charged with high treason and committed to the Tower. No sooner were they there than Lord Lisle set about justifying his boasts to the Council. He was still doing his best to get appointed Lord Lieutenant of Ireland, and there could be no better testimonial to his fitness than that he could command the services of the officers in the Tower. Of Monk there was every hope, for he alone had refused to bind himself not to serve the Parliament, nor were the most enticing offers wanting to tempt him.

Already the New Model Army was in contemplation. Men of all parties saw that nothing decisive would ever be done except by adopting the methods which Monk had urged on the King. A compact mobile field-force, complete and organised in every detail on the Low Country system, must replace the unmanageable mobilised militia with which the war had hitherto been aimlessly dragged on. Cromwell had now definitely come to the front and thrown himself into the task. Except possibly Sir Jacob Astley, who was at Oxford with Charles, there was no one in the kingdom more fitted for the all-important work than Monk. Cromwell, who knew how to choose a man, must have been perfectly aware of his qualifications, even if he had not been as intimate as he was with Lord Lisle. Nor was it from Cromwell alone that the prisoner was tempted. Though all were agreed the weapon must be forged, they were by no means at one as to the hands in which it was to be placed. Independents and Presbyterians were manœuvring for the control. In spite of standing orders members were so constantly visiting the prisoners that the House had strictly to forbid the practice without special leave. The same day a leading Presbyterian was granted permission, and towards the end of October Monk's case was specially referred to the committee of examinations.

But they all mistook their man. He still held the King's commission. The war for which he had engaged was still raging, and the most brilliant offers that could be made him he only regarded as insults. Pressure was even brought to bear, it is said, by a more rigorous confinement, but it was useless, and he indignantly refused his liberty except by a regular cartel.

Days and weeks went by and no exchange came. Although, as he had refused to desert in Ireland, he was not affected by the order which forbade the exchange of the other Irish officers upon any terms, Parliament had no intention of allowing so valuable an officer to get back to the royal camp. In vain Daniel O'Neill urged the King to procure his release for service in Ireland. Charles seems to have done his best. Clarendon says that many attempts were made to exchange him; that one was we know. Care, however, seems to have been taken by his would-be employers not only that these attempts should be unsuccessful, but that Monk should not even hear of them. The wretched colonel thought himself forgotten. His money was gone, and a penniless prisoner in those days was the most miserable of men. Of his annuity fifty pounds was all he had had, and on November 6th, but four months after his committal, he sat down to write an urgent appeal to his brother for another fifty. The letter concludes with a pathetic cry for his release: "I shall entreat you," he says, "to be mindful of me concerning my exchange, for I doubt all my friends have forgotten me. I earnestly entreat you, therefore, if it lies in your power, to remember me concerning my liberty; and so in haste, I rest, your faithful brother, GEORGE MONK."

In haste and in the Tower! But any excuse was good enough with the taciturn soldier if it saved words. And he might have saved them all. Exchange and remittance were alike out of the question with his hard-pressed brother, and as the weary months went by he thought himself indeed deserted. Once out of the very depth of his poverty Charles sent him a hundred pounds —an extraordinary mark of esteem as things went at Oxford then. But that was all. Bitterly he felt the seeming ingratitude, but in spite of all with obstinate loyalty he refused to desert his colours, and sat himself down to forget in the pursuit of literature the fancied wrongs under which he smarted.

Like many other active-minded men before and since, having absolutely nothing to do he determined to write a book. He had before him the example of Lord Vere and his brother-in-arms, Hexham, the literary quarter-master of his old Low Country regiment, and most worthily he followed in their steps. The book is full of vigorous and pithy aphorisms which flash on us the condensed opinions of a man who spoke little and thought much. We can hear, as we read it, the few well-digested words, rugged, blunt, and direct, with which he compelled the attention of councils of war and won the respect and admiration of his men. Its subdued enthusiasm tells us of a genuine soldier reverently devoted to his profession, and looking mournfully from the place apart, where his almost aggressive patriotism had placed him, at the distractions with which his beloved country was torn. It gives us as clearly as though we saw him face to face the key of the character that has been as much misunderstood and abused as any in history. He was an English citizen first, a soldier next, and a politician not at all. Of the real meaning of the strife he was incapable of grasping any conception. For him it was all a mere question of the interior, and in his eyes no question of the interior, not even religion itself, was worth a civil war, or the sacrifice of England's military renown.

He called his work *Observations upon Military and Political Affairs*. The military part is admirable, and shows us the consummate soldier he was. It strikes one of the first notes of modern military science, and takes for its dominant theme the comparatively small part which actual fighting plays in the duties of a general and the success of a campaign. The political observations are more crude but equally characteristic. With the exception of some sagacious remarks on governing a conquered country, they are confined to the methods of preventing civil war. After recommending a strong centralised government, technical education, and uniformity of religion, if it can be obtained without danger, he enunciates those principles which caused him to take the final step at the great crisis of his life. Still under the influence of his Devonshire training he strongly insists on State colonisation as a means whereby sources of weakness may be turned into strength. "But the principal and able remedy," he says, "against civil war is to entertain a foreign war. This chaseth away idleness, setteth all on work, and particularly this giveth satisfaction to ambitious and stirring spirits; it banisheth luxury, maketh your people warlike, and maintaineth you in such reputation amongst your neighbours, that you are the arbitrators of their differences." And it is from this point of view that he expresses his only opinion on the great question that was coming. "A sovereign prince," he lays down, "is more capable to make great and ready conquests than a commonwealth, and especially if he goeth in person into the field."

When the manuscript was complete he gave it to Lord Lisle to take care of, and thus we may be sure that it was from Monk's pen that Cromwell, to whom Lisle would not have omitted to show his treasure, learnt something at least of his knowledge of war.

But literature was not his only consolation. There was another more to his taste and less to his credit. For there used to come to the Tower one Ann Ratsford, the wife of a perfumer who lived at the sign of the Three Spanish Gypsies in the Exchange. By trade she was a milliner, and in that capacity used to look after Monk's linen. She was neither pretty nor well bred; she had a sharp tongue and manners that were not refined. But the colonel was soft-hearted, and she was very kind; the colonel was so handsome and had such a soldierly air, and then all his friends had forgotten him and the perfumer was detestable. So the gloomy walls of the Tower were brightened with an unholy idyl, and thus began the intrigue which was to make a duchess of plain Nan Clarges, the farrier's daughter of the Savoy.

CHAPTER IV

THE PARLIAMENT'S COMMISSION

WHILE Monk lay thus honour-bound in the Tower the New Model had done its work. The war was practically over, and Parliament turned its attention to clearing the prisons. On April 9th, 1646, a return was ordered of all soldiers of fortune then prisoners to the Parliament who were desirous of going abroad, with the intention that on taking the negative oath they should be permitted to do so. Under this order Monk must have applied, and on July 1st he got leave to go beyond the seas.

Besides the oath there was a further condition that he was to leave the country within a month of his release, but his friends seem to have had influence enough to get the time extended. With the close of the war Parliament was able to devote its energies to Ireland, and each party was scheming to appoint the Lord Lieutenant, in order to secure for itself the prestige of avenging the Protestant blood that had been shed. During Monk's imprisonment the situation there had changed considerably. Ormonde still held Dublin and the greater part of Leinster for the King, but Lord Inchiquin in a fit of pique had gone over to the Parliament, and from Cork was administering Munster as president in its name.

The Scotch in the Ulster garrisons and plantations were also on the side of the Parliament. The rest of the island was in the hands of the Papal Nuncio, and recognised no authority either of King or Parliament. He had succeeded in uniting the Anglo-Irish under Preston and the native Irish under Owen O'Neill into one ultra-Catholic party, with vague aims at an independent state under the protectorate of Spain or the Pope.

Parliament saw something must be done to keep Inchiquin from returning to his allegiance and joining Ormonde ; and being still unable to agree upon a definite appointment, they determined to send out Lord Lisle for a year. He immediately offered the command of his regiment to Monk. There was now no reason why he should not accept it. The war for which he had engaged was at an end, and the new service that was offered to him was one which he had been bred to think as noble as a crusade. It was against an enemy in open rebellion against England and in secret league with Spain.

But though perfectly willing to accept the negative oath, to which as a merely military precaution he had no objection, he utterly refused to take the Covenant. Till he did he was not qualified for a parliamentary commission.

By the end of September, however, Ormonde found it was impossible to hold out much longer, and rather than let Dublin fall into the hands of the Catholics, he offered to surrender it to the Parliament. At the same time he urged them to send out Monk and the Irish officers to take command of the army of occupation. The difficulties about the recusant colonel's appointment began to vanish like magic. The Presbyterians, who, it must be remembered, were in theory Royalist, and practically becoming so every day in a greater degree, naturally were only too glad to accept a nomination of Ormonde's. Monk was sent for by the Irish committee of the Council of State sitting at Derby House. There he pledged his honour that he would faithfully serve the Parliament in the Irish war, and announced himself ready to start at a day's notice. What was said about the Covenant is a mystery, but the committee reported to the House that he was ready to take it. That he did not take it is certain, for this was the chief ground on which the Ulster-Scotch quarrelled with him three years afterwards. It is difficult even to believe that honest George said he was ready to do so. The ambiguous expression looks strangely like an ingenious piece of jockeying on the part of Lisle, who was a member of the Derby House committee, to make it easy for the Presbyterians to consent to Monk's appointment. At all events it had the desired effect, and with only one dissentient voice it was voted that Colonel Monk should be employed as the committee directed.

Lord Lisle was less successful in his own case. Not till Christmas did he get his route, and still there were obstacles which prevented him sailing till the middle of February. Even then he did not go to Dublin. Ormonde and the parliamentary commissioners had not been able to agree on the details of the surrender, and Lisle had to land in Cork. It was the 21st of the month before he reached his command, and his commission would expire on April 15th. Barely two months remained of his term

of office, and that time was spent in incessant wrangling
between Lord Inchiquin and the newly arrived officers.
It is needless to say that the expedition was an entire
failure, and on the first of May Monk and his friends
found themselves once more back in London.

It shows plainly how Monk had kept himself clear
of any political taint that he did not share in his chief's
fall. The force which had been sent to occupy Dublin
on the first overtures of Ormonde had been ordered on
to Ulster pending the completion of the negotiations.
On the eventual signing of the treaty of rendition, as a
strong force was on its way from England, only a small
part of the original army of occupation had been ordered
to Dublin, and an officer was required to command the
regiments which remained in Ulster. Everything pointed
to Monk as the man. His appointment was strongly urged
by his friends in the House, and probably by Cromwell
himself, and in July he was gratified with a commission
as Major-General over all the forces both Scotch and
English, in the counties of Down and Antrim and all
those parts of Ulster which were not in the command
of Sir Charles Coote.

Michael Jones was supreme in Dublin, and with a
man like Monk to second him he soon set the tide
running back. Early in August he inflicted a crushing
defeat on Preston, and O'Neill alone remained to be
dealt with. But that was different. He was a wary
old Low Country officer who had been long in the
Spanish service. He knew his power lay in guerilla
warfare, and nothing would entrap him into an engagement. He was a foe worthy of the new commanders'
steel, but they knew the game as well as he. All

E

through August and the two following months Monk
and Jones were raiding up and down, sometimes in
concert, sometimes apart, burning, ravaging, plundering,
and collecting provisions.

Such work was all that Monk could do with the forces
at his command, and he did it well.   To hold his ground
till the great expedition, which was in contemplation for
·the conquest of Ireland, could start was all he could hope ;
and till one party or the other got the upper hand in
the English Parliament that would never be.   So while
politicians at home were scheming as to who should set
the King on his throne again and the sterner voices were
beginning to mutter darkly that it was not there he
must find his rest, honest George in his matter-of-fact
business-like way was quietly busy with the duty of his
place.   For him the growing dissensions amongst his
paymasters were nothing, except in so far as they found
them too absorbing to make time to send him money
and supplies.

Till the questions of the King and the command of the
army were settled things were at a deadlock, and Monk
was thrown on his own resources.   It was now that he
began to show how great these resources were, and how
to the reckless courage and strategic sagacity of the
soldier he added all the qualities that go to make the
successful proconsul.   In his province he was an autocrat.
He had a commission to execute martial law, an extraordinary mark of confidence in those days, and governed
despotically in a state of siege.   Yet no administration
had ever been more generally popular.   So just or
judicious were his decisions on every point that came
before him that long after he was gone they were quoted

as unassailable precedents. The Protestants began to
feel the colony had got a new start in life.

Nor in the duties of judge and governor did he relax
the unsleeping vigilance of the general. Time after time
O'Neill attempted a raid, but it was only to fall into the
midst of a force that scattered his troops like chaff; and
when he succeeded in regaining the desolate fastnesses
from which he had issued, it was but to hear how Monk's
soldiers had swept down in his absence on some distant
spot and carried off a precious booty of cattle and pro-
vender. For honest practical George was far too much
of a soldier not to know the value of spies, and he used
them unscrupulously. O'Neill could not move hand or
foot before an iron grip was on him. Splendid soldier
as he was he had met his match, and never could he get
within striking distance of his enemy's magazines.

Nor was this all. For while the Irish were kept at a
distance in a state of starvation the English soldiers were
digging pay and provision out of the desolation, where
once the wretched partisans of O'Neill had had their
homes. And so by a happy combination of the patient
industry of the ploughman and the daring activity of the
mosstrooper Monk made the war support itself, a thing
as strange as it was palatable to the authorities at home ;
and while he thus delighted his masters he no less attached
his troops to him by his judicious distribution of loot, as
well as by keeping an open house to which every officer
had at all times a hearty welcome. His maxim was to
"mingle love with the severity of his discipline," believing
that "they that cannot be induced to serve for love will
never be forced to serve for fear."

But troubles were at hand. The province was no bed

of roses, or if it were, the thorns grew faster than the
flowers as the breath of party strife began to reach it in
fitful gusts. Ever since Ormonde had left Dublin he had
been busily engaged with the King's friends, who were
taking advantage of the growing royalism of the Presbyterians to form a new combination against the Parliament. In Scotland and Munster lay their chief hopes
of backing a rising in England, and so well did Ormonde
play his part that in April, 1648, the Independent officers
under Inchiquin found it necessary to make a desperate
attempt to save the province by seizing Cork and Youghal.
The plot failed, Inchiquin at once showed his hand for
the King, and Munster was lost to the Parliament. This
was followed at the end of the month by a declaration
from Scotland in favour of Charles, and the mobilisation
of the forces of the Northern Kingdom.

The second Civil War had begun, and Inchiquin
sought to improve his position by concluding a cessation
and alliance with Clanrickarde and his Irish party, and by
secretly negotiating with the Scots in Ulster. Already
Monk had had sufficient trouble with them. At the outbreak of the Rebellion in 1641 Munroe had sailed from
Scotland to the assistance of the old Scotch settlers.
Since then he and his New Scotch, as they were called,
had succeeded by their overbearing conduct in making
themselves extremely unpopular with the Old Scotch,
and Monk had plenty to do to hold the balance between
them. Now there was a new complication. The Old
Scotch party was as yet decidedly anti-Royalist. They
had never forgiven Charles for his attempted alliance
with O'Neill and the execrated authors of the Ulster
massacres. It was then with Munroe and the New

Scotch that Inchiquin sought to deal, and not in vain.
Munroe adhered to the coalition, but his adhesion was
kept a profound secret till the time came for action.
The idea seems to have been that so soon as Ormonde
arrived from France to take command in Ireland
Monk should be seized. No attempt appears to have
been made to tamper with him.   Though Ormonde
tempted Coote and Jones, he knew Monk too well to be
ignorant that his sting could only be drawn by violence.

The danger was extreme, and the fate of the cause
hung in a balance.   Besides the three English officers,
O'Neill and his Nationalists were all in Ireland that
were not in arms for the King.   Across St. George's
Channel the Scots were already over the border with a
force so formidable that none could foresee the issue
when they and Cromwell met.   Munroe held Carrickfergus and Belfast.   Ormonde was on his way from
France, and if ever Charles had a chance it was now.
The fate of Ireland hung for the moment on Monk.
With Ulster in Ormonde's hands O'Neill's last chance
was gone, and Coote and Jones single-handed could
never hold out.

But from Monk's vigilance the danger could not be
concealed, and for him to know was to act.   He saw his
duty, he saw his chance, and sharp and sudden he struck
his blow.   One day in the middle of September Munroe
was in his quarters ready for the moment of action, when
suddenly there was a confused alarm, and before the
Scotchman well knew what it meant he found himself a
prisoner in the hands of Monk, and the towns of Belfast
and Carrickfergus in possession of the English and the
Old Scotch.

The bells were ringing for Cromwell's overwhelming victory at Preston when the news came that Ulster was safe as yet and Ireland reprieved. In an outburst of gratitude the Houses ordered a public thanksgiving, voted the hero of the hour a letter of thanks, appointed him Governor of Belfast, gave him the disposal of Carrickfergus and a gratuity of £500, and resolved to try and pay all his men's arrears. From that moment his fortune was made. The Independents were now supreme. For them his blow had been struck, and people began to forget he had ever drawn sword for the King.

Still in spite of his success his position in Ireland was anything but enviable. The Parliament was triumphant in England, but the account was still open between the Independents and the Presbyterians, and until it was closed little could be done for the relief of Ireland. Even when Cromwell had settled it with a squad of musketeers, and the execution of Charles had removed the great obstacle to a permanent settlement, much remained to be done before the great Irish Expedition could start. For the moment history turned on the race for Ireland, and a close race it was. The execution of Charles was followed by the Scots of Ulster declaring unanimously against the Republic. Coote was shut up in Derry, and Monk with the greatest difficulty escaped a surprise, and took refuge in Dundalk.[1] The situation was growing desperate indeed. The Royalists held the whole country with the exception of the ground which was covered by the guns of the garrisons, or occupied by O'Neill's Nationalists. The English Expedition was far

[1] Edw. Butler to Rupert, *Hist. MSS. Rep. IX.*, pt. 2, p. 440 b.

from ready, and Ormonde was leaving no stone unturned
to make the whole island his own before it could sail.
Again he was tempting Jones and Coote, though again
he did not waste time on Monk. He was offering baits
to O'Neill. He was urging the new King to come over
and complete the work with his presence. So well was
he working that in February the Papal Nuncio fled,
leaving him in possession of the field. O'Neill's sup-
porters began to desert. Every day the country which
the Ulster chief could call his own grew less and less.
The fall of Dublin and the other English garrisons began
to stare the English Council in the face. Something
must be done to stave off the end yet a little while, and
the strangest and most obscure of all that time is the
story of the means the Council employed for the work.

CHAPTER V

ABOUT the middle of February, 1649, Dr. Winstad, a worthy English Catholic physician residing at Rouen, went to welcome his friend, Sir Kenelm Digby, who had just ridden into the town on his way from Paris with several young gentlemen in his company. He was surprised to find amongst the party a "wry-necked fellow" with manners to match, and was pained to see his respected friend making a great fuss of the stranger although he did not scruple to "openly dispute against the blessed Trinity." He was certainly not fit company for Catholic gentlemen. But worse was yet to come. The doctor was soon informed that the wry-necked scoffer was none other than Scoutmaster-general Watson, the Head of the Intelligence Department of the New Model Army, and the whole party were possessed of passes to go into England, which he had procured for them from headquarters.

Thoroughly alarmed, the doctor wrote off to Secretary Nicholas to warn him that a desperate plot was on foot. Lord Byron happened to be there, too, on his way to Paris to urge the King's departure for Ireland, and just as he was getting into the saddle the news came to his

ears. Sir Kenelm and his young gentlemen had kept
their secret ill, and so soon as Byron reached Caen he
was able to send off post-haste to Ormonde a warning
that the ultra-Catholics were conspiring with the Independents to abolish hereditary monarchy in return for
toleration of their own religion. He begged him to
keep his eyes open in Ireland, where the plot might
have very serious consequences. Secretary Nicholas
caught the alarm and warned Ormonde of a possible
alliance between O'Neill and the English officers.

At a moment when the great Presbyterian body was
in the last stage of exasperation at the expulsion of its
members from the House by Cromwell it seemed almost
incredible that the Independents should dare to try and
strengthen their position by the very scheme which
ruined Charles. Yet it was all true. In spite of the
storm which Glamorgan's attempt had raised less than
three years ago, the Council of State was secretly holding out its hand to the blood-stained savages who were
the very authors of the massacres about to be avenged.
Such at least was the sentiment which the name of
O'Neill and the Ulster Nationalists called up in England,
and yet the risk must be run.

Ever since the preceding August, Jones had been in
communication with O'Neill. An emissary of Monk's
had been caught in secret negotiation with an officer
from the Irish army. In October the Nuncio had
announced to his superiors that there was a danger
of the Nationalists joining with the Independents and
"steeping the kingdom in blood." How far the
proceedings were authorised from headquarters it is
impossible to say. All we know is that for some

time past there had been strange rumours about in
London and mysterious goings and comings of Catholic
gentlemen whose passports were always in order. But
now Ormonde had got definite information to go upon,
and he acted with his usual address. His attempts to
gain Jones and Coote were redoubled, and offers were
made which seem to have shaken O'Neill himself. Monk
was not spared. The Ulster Presbyterians, who had
revolted from him, were set on to appeal to him with
the only reasons to which his ears were open, and he
found himself face to face with the moral dilemma that
was to haunt him year after year till the Restoration
brought him rest. To whom was the duty of his place?
The Presbyterians argued that they could not recognise
any authority but that of a covenanted Parliament, and
urged Monk to join them in supporting their position.
Monk replied that he considered himself bound by his
commission to stand by the *de facto* authority in England,
which was the Purged Parliament and the Council of
State, and demanded why they refused to do the same.
They replied that the *de facto* government was not a
lawful authority. It existed merely by virtue of its
coercion of the lawful authority which was Parliament
as it existed before Pride's Purge; and as an ultimatum
they required him to take the Covenant and obey no
orders but those of the Council of War at Belfast. Monk
flatly refused. It was a difficult question. But his
notions of duty pointed clearly to the thorny path of
resistance, and he determined to defend Dundalk to the
last.

Meanwhile the Independent plot had been maturing.
Towards the end of March an agent from O'Neill had

appeared in London and managed, probably through
Jones's recommendation, to communicate with the Council
of State. The Council refused to receive him, but appointed a secret committee to hear what he had to say.
The effect of their report was that the game was too
dangerous, and the agent was ordered to leave London.
Still if the game were too dangerous for the Council,
Cromwell knew it was too good not to carry on a while
longer, and there is little doubt that Jones received from
him some secret instructions to that effect, which were
communicated to Monk. It was absolutely necessary for
the success of the coming expedition to Ireland that the
Scotch and northern Royalists should be kept from joining hands with Ormonde, Clanrickarde, and Inchiquin,
and so completing the investment of Dublin. The maimed
and shattered forces of Monk and O'Neill were all that
held them apart.

O'Neill for some time had been in receipt of ammunition and supplies from the English officers, and Cromwell
either now or not long afterwards was giving him regular
pay ; but this would no longer do. At the end of April
O'Neill wrote a Latin letter to Monk urging him to press
the Council once more to conclude a treaty on the terms
his agent had unsuccessfully offered. But for this there
was no time. A strong force was advancing upon O'Neill
under Lord Castlehaven. It was a crisis in view of which
Monk may or may not have had his instructions. At
any rate he replied to O'Neill's letter asking what his
terms were, and then after a short negotiation concluded
with him on May 8th an armistice for three months, in
order to give time for communication with England.
The convention included a general defensive and offen-

sive alliance between them against Ormonde for the time,
provided always that no agreement was to be made by
either with any one in arms against the Parliament.

The effect was immediate. The Scots lost heart and
ceased to press Monk, and he had leisure to forward
O'Neill's new terms to England. How far he knew
Cromwell was behind "the special friends and well-
wishers to this service" who were advising him is uncertain. At any rate he was aware the Council must
not know all, and that Cromwell was the man to address. So he sat down and wrote a long letter thanking
the general for his many favours, and telling him the
whole story of how his own desperate position and the
necessity of keeping O'Neill from accepting Ormonde's
terms had decided him to take the step he had. "I do
not think fit," he continues, "to signify this to the Council
of State, but do wholly refer the business to you either
to make further use of it, or else to move it, or as you
conceive most fit to be done. Since there was great
necessity for me to do it, I hope it will beget no ill construction." And so he concludes beseeching Cromwell
"to continue his good opinion" towards him.

It was well for Monk he took the cautious line he
did. Up to the end of the first week in May the Council
had been sending him flattering letters of encouragement
and promises of ships, provisions, and everything he
asked for. A large sum of money was actually on ship-
board consigned to him. When suddenly the day before
the armistice was concluded a messenger was galloping
down to the coast to stop it. Special precautions were
taken to prevent the reason of this sudden order being
known, and we can only guess that something of Monk's

purpose or secret instructions had leaked out. But some one there was to smooth things over, and before the week was out the money was on its way again with a letter addressed by the Council to Monk thanking him for his services and integrity.

Whatever it was that Cromwell thought most fit to be done, it was not to reprimand Monk. His vast preparations for the conquest of Ireland were approaching completion, and by the armistice he gained the delay he required. All that was wanted was to keep the treaty secret till he was well on his way, and then he could do without it. Meanwhile Monk was allowed to believe that his conduct was approved by the authorities at home, and told to keep the whole matter a profound secret.

It was not long before he had to test the value of his treaty. Early in June Ormonde had concentrated all his forces and advanced to Dublin. Taking up a position there he detached Inchiquin to take Drogheda and Trim, and so open up communication with his allies in the north. At the end of the month Drogheda fell and Inchiquin advanced to besiege Dundalk. Monk at once sent to O'Neill to come to his assistance. O'Neill replied that he could do nothing for want of ammunition. Monk was ready to supply the want, and told his ally to send up a strong convoy to receive it. All went well till the party was returning laden with supplies. So hospitably had they been treated in Dundalk that most of them were drunk. Indeed no precautions seem to have been taken to prevent a surprise, possibly because O'Neill was still coquetting with Ormonde, and had some understanding that he should be allowed to get ammunition from Monk. At any rate before his men reached their camp a detachment of Inchiquin's army fell upon them and cut them to pieces. Hardly a man escaped, the whole of the train was captured, and so great was the panic in O'Neill's quarters when the news of the disaster came, that the whole army fled in disorder to Longford and left Dundalk to its fate.

It was a trying moment for Monk, and one in which the blunt narrow-minded soldier of fortune stands out in his fearlessness and staunch self-reliance a figure almost heroic. The end for which he had been striving so long was nearly gained. Any time within the next few weeks Cromwell might set foot in Ireland. The army was gathered at Milford. The Lord Lieutenant had left London. The race for the key of England was now neck and neck. One more struggle and success might still be won. So like a true man Monk resolved at all hazards to cling to his charge till he could cling no more.

His troops were his only fear. Arrears and the O'Neill treaty had been a sore trial to their devotion, but still they were the only tools he had. Calling them about him he told them what he meant to do, and begged that, if any there feared to stand by him, he would be gone. A single man stepped from the ranks and said he could not fight by the side of Popish rebels red with Protestant blood. He was dismissed with a safe-conduct, and the rest pledged themselves to stand by their beloved commander till the last.

It is sad to tell how night cooled their courage. Next day when Inchiquin appeared before the walls the sight was more than their conscientious scruples and empty pockets could endure. Wholesale they deserted

to the enemy, till Monk at last was left with but seventeen faithful out of all his force. Still he would have
held out, though resistance then meant certain death.
Fortunately the seventeen faithful were not so obstinate,
and he was but one against them. By main force they
compelled him to surrender. Inchiquin gave him handsome terms. They were simply that he should be allowed
to dispose of himself and his property as he pleased,
and in pursuance of them he presently sailed for
England.

But his troubles instead of being ended were only
begun. No sooner was he landed at Chester than he
found public opinion in a high state of agitation over his
armistice. He was interviewed by excited politicians :
he was eagerly asked what induced him to make so
monstrous an alliance ; but little could be made of him.
The cautious, taciturn soldier must have been a difficult
man to interview, and to every inquisitive attack he
replied that he had the warrant of his superiors for what
he had done. He had obeyed his orders, he had done
his duty, and he had no fear of the consequences ; nor
did it concern him whether the treaty was justifiable or
not.

Once ashore he lost no time in hurrying on to Milford
Haven to report himself to Cromwell, who as Lord Lieutenant was his immediate superior. There he found
matters worse even than at Chester. The soldiers had
got wind of the unlucky armistice and were deserting in
large numbers. They had enlisted to avenge innocent
Protestant blood, and found themselves asked to join
hands with the monsters who had shed it. The stories
of the massacres were still believed, and feeling ran very

high. One of Milton's first commissions from the Government had been aimed at involving their opponents in the execration with which Ormonde's peace with the Irish Papists was regarded, and men's ears were still ringing with his tremendous invective against the Ulster Scots for joining hands with a man who had so stained himself with the touch of Antichrist. It was a time when Cromwell must have repented his patriotic resolve to command the Irish army. He well knew the danger he ran in leaving London. He was sure his Presbyterian and Cavalier enemies would leave no stone unturned to damage him and his party. And here at the very outset the weapon which Milton had been wielding with such deadly effect was placed within their reach. The connection between the Independents and the Papists once exposed, there would be a resistless outcry such as had greeted the Glamorgan disclosures, and the cause of individual liberty, of toleration, of independency would be lost for ever. Whatever the cost the truth must not transpire.

Such must have been Cromwell's thoughts as Monk was announced. What would we not give to see that meeting now, to see those two men, so alike and yet so widely different, face to face at a moment so dramatic! Cromwell with the fierce earnestness that carried all before it telling his friend that no more must be said about the warrant of his superiors, that on his own shoulders he must for the sake of the good cause take the blame; telling him how he had laid his confidential letter and O'Neill's terms before the Council, and how they had voted entire disapproval of the whole scheme, and had not even dared to put it before Parliament. And then the honest soldier, hurt to be so deserted, but yet borne down by the resistless personality of his commander, consenting at last for high reasons of state to lie. He who, as Clarendon said, was never suspected of dissimulation in all his life passed his word to lie, and Cromwell knew—none better than he —a man that was to be trusted.

So much is all we can gather of that meeting on which so much depended. No sooner was it over than the scapegoat was hurried off to London. No time was to be lost. The rising storm must be allayed before it got beyond control, and Cromwell could not sail till he knew the end. There was a magic sword lying almost in his enemies' grasp, and till it was removed he could not leave —no, not for all Ireland.

Armed with letters to Cromwell's friends Monk arrived in London early in August. "They should commit him to the Tower," said one when he knew he had come. "Better commit the Tower to him," was the reply, for Cromwell's letters made friends plentiful. It would even appear that Oliver's partisans in the Council had a hint to make things as smooth for Monk as was consistent with their own safety, and very cleverly they went about it.

It was of course now necessary that they should make a report of the whole affair to Parliament. The secrecy which had been ordered in reference to the matter was removed by vote. Monk was sent for and examined as to his reasons for taking the course he had. He replied without hesitation that it was an act of military necessity, and what he had done was entirely on his own responsibility in expectation of the Council's confirmation. Nothing could be more satisfactory. He was ordered to draw up a report explaining the position and to attend the House with it on the following Wednesday. He was further informed that the Council disapproved of the whole matter from beginning to end; all which things were next day embodied in formal resolutions for report to the House, and it is worth remarking that this was the only occasion during the whole month on which Lord Lisle attended the Council.

On the 10th Monk went down to the House with his report. Jones's despatch announcing his great victory over Ormonde and the safety of Dublin had just arrived. After it had been read Monk was called to the bar and presented his report. But the House was not so easily satisfied as the Council. The Opposition were still strong, and they felt they were being hoodwinked. Monk's letter to Cromwell had been laid on the table with the rest of the papers, and in it was the fatal admission that he had been advised by some well-wishers to the cause. The House demanded to know who those persons were.

It must have been an anxious moment for many there as the Speaker's voice ceased and silence fell upon the eager throng while they listened for Monk's reply. Who could tell he would stand staunch at that trying moment?

"I did it," said Monk with his stolid air, "on my own score without the advice of any other persons. Only formerly I had some discourse of Colonel Jones, and he told me if I could keep off Owen Rowe and Ormonde from joining it would be a good service."

"Had you any advice or direction," continued the Speaker, "from Parliament, or the Council, or the Lord Lieutenant of Ireland, or any person here to do it?"

"Neither from Parliament," answered Monk categorically, "nor the Council, nor the Lord Lieutenant, nor any person here had I any advice or direction. I did it on my own score for the preservation of the English interest there, and it has had some fruits accordingly."

There was no denying that. Lying on the table before them was Jones's despatch, in which he attributed his great victory to the fact that Ormonde had been compelled to detach Inchiquin to oppose O'Neill. Monk was ordered to withdraw, and a long debate ensued. The Opposition felt their weapon was being filched from their hands, and they argued long for a vote of censure, while Monk waited anxiously without. At last the question was put, "That this House do approve the proceeding of Colonel Monk?" The House divided, and the motion was lost. Then it was put that "the House do utterly disapprove, and that the innocent blood which hath been shed is so fresh in the memory of this House that the House doth detest and abhor the thoughts of any closing with any party of Popish rebels there who have had their hands in shedding that blood." But an amendment was moved by adding words to the motion that Monk's conduct was excusable on the ground of necessity. In this form it was carried, and Monk was safe.

Cromwell had won. He was still lying in Milford Haven. The money for which he had stayed had been sent off a fortnight ago : the corn-ships had gone some days before ; yet still he tarried. On August 12th the news of the momentous vote reached him, and next day he sailed. If it was not this that loosed his moorings the good tidings came at least with strange opportuneness, and permitted him to leave England with his greatest anxiety allayed.

The victory was indeed complete. At the end of the

week the official press came out full of flattering expressions about Monk. A full account was published by authority for the information or delusion of the public. In vain the opposition "Man in the Moon" railed, and said the whole thing was a "blindation." The public were satisfied with the result, and the incident was at an end.[1]

And now for the last time in his life Monk knew what it was to be out of employment. His brother, Colonel Thomas Monk, the zealous Cavalier, had recently been killed by a fall from his horse, and George seems to have used his leisure to go down to Potheridge and take possession of the family estates, which fell to him as heir-in-tail. It was probably at this time that he became fully impressed with the abilities of his kinsman Mr. Morice, who was afterwards to influence his career so profoundly. This remarkable man, scholar, historian, recluse, and man of business, had been managing the Grenville property with great skill ever since Monk's uncle, Sir Bevil, had been killed at the battle of Lansdowne, and the colonel found he could not do better than commit his own property to the same stewardship.

But that it was not only in this manner that he enjoyed his repose and consoled himself for the way the Government had treated him is only too clear. For it was in this year that the frail Mrs. Ratsford was separated from her husband.

[1] Rinuccini to Card. Pauzirolo, October 31st, November 9th and 29th, 1648; *Memoirs*, p. 441; Walker's *Hist. of Independency*, vol. ii. pp. 150, 233-248; *Capt. Stewart's MSS., Hist. MSS. Rep. X.*, iv. p. 82, Col. Moore to Gen. Monck; "The Declaration of the British on the North of Ireland, etc.," April 9th, 1649; *Br. Mus.* E$\frac{456}{15}$; Council Book during May and August 1649; Gilbert's app. to *Aphorismal Discovery; Ormonde Letters* and *Com. Journ.*

CHAPTER VI

MONK had hardly time to weary of his inactivity before
a new storm burst in the north. Scotland had taken
to herself a covenanted King, and an invasion was resolved upon by the English Parliament. Cromwell was
recalled from Ireland, and in June, 1650, to the confusion
of the Presbyterian opposition, he was voted to the
command of the army. He at once sent for Monk to
assist him in the organisation of his forces, and promised
him a regiment.

The significance of this it is hard to exaggerate.
When we remember how fastidious Cromwell was about
the private character of the men he worked with, it cannot but impress us with the extraordinary sense he must
have had of his obligations to Monk. The highest
military abilities would never have induced him to
employ a man who was living in open contempt of the
seventh commandment. It was an offence of such gravity
at that time that it had been recently made capital.
Yet Cromwell was determined his trusty friend should
have his reward, and that in spite of the difficulty
of finding him a regiment. The command of Bright's,
which lay at Alnwick, was vacant, but a dangerous

spirit of democracy and autonomy was growing in the army. Bright's had been one of the victorious regiments at Nantwich. They had to be asked if they would accept Monk for colonel, and they refused. "We took him prisoner," they cried, "at Nantwich not long since, and he will betray us," and ominously enough Lambert, with whom the last great struggle was to be, was chosen in his stead. From that moment the two most celebrated of Cromwell's lieutenants were doomed to an incessant rivalry.

But Cromwell was not to be thwarted. As there was no regiment for his friend, he made one. At Newcastle lay Sir Arthur Haslerig's renowned Blue-Coats, and at Berwick was Colonel Fenwick with his newly raised Northumberland regiment. The field-force which had been voted for Cromwell was complete, but in his masterful way he drew five companies from each of these regiments and made up a new one for Monk. Then he laconically informed the House what he had done, and coolly requested that the new regiment should be taken on the establishment and the two weakened garrisons recruited. Like lambs the Government consented, and so in lawless birth, a reward for service that none dared name, began the famous Coldstream Guards.

The staff-appointment which Monk held was that of acting lieutenant-general of the Ordnance. Cromwell would doubtless have preferred to see him sergeant-major-general—an appointment which in those days of amateur soldiering it was usually thought necessary to fill with a soldier of fortune—that as chief of the staff he might supply the technical shortcomings of the commander-in-chief. It was, however, already occupied by

Lambert, whose training as a lawyer can hardly have
qualified him for the proper discharge of its complex
duties. Indeed more than once, in cases of extreme
difficulty, we shall see that Monk had to take over his
work, and thus intensify the antipathy which marked
their relations from the first.

It is impossible here to repeat the oft-told tale of the
Dunbar campaign; which is the more to be regretted as
Monk's share in it has never been done justice to.
Cromwell had excellent reasons for not saying too much
about him in despatches; and Hodgson, the other best
known authority, being in Lambert's regiment, studiously
keeps in the background the rival of his idolised colonel.
Yet it is certain that no voice had so much weight with
Cromwell as Monk's, and he was consulted at every point.
Up to Dunbar, too, the lion's share of the active operations fell upon him. The artillery duels by which it was
sought to goad Leslie into an engagement were under
his direction, and it was he who took the castles of
Colinton and Redhall during Cromwell's attempt to turn
the Scotch position before Edinburgh.

During the terrible retreat on Dunbar it is hardly too
much to say his consummate technical skill saved the
army from destruction. More dead than alive the
remnants of Cromwell's splendid force had reached
Haddington. Sick, shattered, and harassed to death
with incessant marching through the rain and mire, they
seemed now an easy prey. About midnight an attack on
the rear-guard had been repulsed, but the position was
none the less desperate. Leslie was at their heels bent
on destroying them before they could reach their ships.
He was out-marching them to the right on a line parallel

to their own, and it was certain that with the first glimpse
of daylight he would be upon them. Yet it seemed
impossible to do anything. A Scotch mist was driving
across them and the darkness was absolutely impenetrable. As they stood in the ranks the soldiers could
hardly see their right and left hand files. Yet Monk
undertook to draw the army up in line of battle fronting
to its true right. It was Lambert's duty as major-
general; and it must have been a rough blow to his
vanity that his rival was not only allowed to undertake
a task for which his own experience was inadequate, but
that he succeeded in what seemed an impossibility. For
succeed he did. By feeling or instinct he set about
the work, of which we can now have little conception.
Complicated mathematical calculations were involved;
foot had to be mingled with horse, and pikemen with
musketeers. But all this was child's play to Monk.
The dismal morning broke, and there Leslie saw facing
him a line of battle, perfect in every distance and resting
on Gladsmuir and Haddington, with a swollen tributary
of the Tyne to protect its front. Without hesitation
the Scotch general declined the action, and hurried on
to secure Cockburnspath and cut off Cromwell from
Berwick.

We must pass on to the evening of September
2nd. In Dunbar the spiritless supper at the head-
quarters' mess was over and Cromwell was walking with
Lambert hoping against hope for a chance of escape.
But the position was unchanged. There was still the
swollen Brock roaring along its impassable channel in
heavy spate from the right to where it joined the sea on
the extreme left: there was the narrow stretch of

meadow beyond; and then the hills, where dimly in the
gathering gloom the Scottish host lay out and penned
them in past hope. Suddenly there was a movement.
The Scotch were beginning to draw down from the hills,
the horse on their right flank were taking ground towards
the sea. It was clear Leslie meant to attack on the morrow where on the English left the Berwick road crossed
the Brock. The manœuvre was difficult. In the narrow
piece of level ground that was available between the hills
and the burn it would take long to execute, and until
it was complete the right flank of the Scots which had
hitherto been secure in the difficult ground about Cockburnspath was exposed. Leslie must be attacked when
his movement was half-done. It was a desperate chance,
but the only one against his overwhelming numbers.

Lambert agreed with Cromwell's suggestion, but the
General would not decide without Monk's opinion. He
was probably busy superintending the embarkation of
his heavy guns, but he was quickly found and received
the idea favourably. All depended on the success of the
first attack. The ford must be seized before Leslie was
ready to cross, and then the Scotch line as it lay between the hills and the burn taking ground to the right
might be rolled up like a scroll. There must be no
thought of repulse; he offered to lead the foot in
person, and again he was given the post that Lambert
as major-general ought to have filled.

The Council of War was assembled at once, and
Monk demonstrated to the colonels the practicability
of Cromwell's idea. The attack was decided on, and
the first glimmer of dawn saw Monk standing beside
the burn, half-pike in hand, at the head of his regiment

of foot.[1] All was ready to begin, but Lambert, who was
to lead the attack at the head of the horse, was away,
to Cromwell's annoyance, worrying about Monk's guns
with which he had suggested a feint should be made
upon the Scots' left. Valuable time was lost, but at last
he came, and the horse dashed across the ford followed by
Monk in support. A desperate hand-to-hand fight ensued.
For an hour the thing hung in a balance. The flower of
the Scotch regiments was there, and the resistance they
offered was worthy of their reputation. But regiment
after regiment poured over from the Dunbar side, ever
inclining to the left till the Scotch right was overlapped.
All this time Monk was fighting desperately at pike's
length with a regiment that would not break. But now
as the rout of the out-flanked regiments exposed it to the
horse it had to go with the rest, and then the day was
won. Galled by the guns and small-shot from across the
swollen burn, the Scots' left and centre, incapable of
reaching their enemy, would stand no longer. As the
beaten right fell back upon them, rolling up the line as

[1] Monk's biographers give him the credit of originating the
whole movement, but in the face of Cromwell's despatch that is
hardly possible. Heath (*Chron.* p. 274) is probably right when he
says that "at the general's request he did draw and design the
whole fight and embattle the army," but he cannot be trusted in
assigning the whole credit of the victory to Monk. Hodgson, of
course, attributes everything to Lambert, and states that at the
end of the Council one stepped up and asked that he (Lambert)
might have the conduct of the army that day—an assertion which
is only credible on the supposition that Cromwell had previously
taken the conduct out of his major-general's hands. In view of
Monk's recent feat at Haddington this is not unlikely, and Lambert
may well have been given the post of honour at the head of the
attack to reconcile him to the slight.

they came, a panic ensued. Throwing down their arms they fairly ran, nor stopped till they reached Edinburgh.

The fall of Edinburgh Castle ended the campaign of 1650. Monk had been appointed governor of the city, and with the duties of his office and the preparations for the next campaign he was occupied during the winter. By February, however, in the following year, he was at active work again. Tantallon Castle was his first care, and by the aid of the splendid siege-train he had organised he battered the ancient stronghold of the Douglas into submission in forty-eight hours: Blackness Castle on the Forth followed in March; and thus by the time spring had fairly begun the way was cleared for the real object of the campaign, and Monk's services were rewarded with the substantive rank in which he had been acting.

Leslie during the winter had reorganised his army, and was occupying an intrenched position at Torwood, to the north of Falkirk, covering Stirling. Beyond him the government was being carried on in security at Perth. The Torwood position was far too strong for a direct attack to be risked. Every endeavour to turn it or to tempt Leslie to leave failed, and yet it was imperative that he should be dislodged.

Who suggested the daring manœuvre by which the end was at last achieved we do not know. At this time Monk was higher in his commander's counsels than ever. Brilliant tactician as he was, Cromwell had hitherto given little evidence of far-sighted strategy. He was not a trained soldier, and Lambert was only a talented civilian like himself. Deane had had no scientific training in the continental school, nor did he join

the army till May. Indeed Monk was the only professional soldier on the staff at the time the manœuvre
was projected. But if Cromwell was no professional
soldier he had the military instinct too highly developed
not to know his own shortcomings, and to appreciate
at its full value the consummate technical knowledge
of his new adviser. The few words that fell blunt and
sure from the taciturn soldier of fortune had more
weight in the Council of War than all the rest together.
At any rate we may be sure the movement was the
result of Cromwell's and Monk's reconnaissance of
Leslie's position at Stirling in September, and that it
was worked out by Monk on his return to Edinburgh.
For in November a requisition went up to the Council
of State for the flotilla of flat-bottomed boats which the
contemplated operation required.

It was known at the English headquarters that there
was a party about the King who were urging an advance
into England. The plan had much to recommend it,
and Cromwell determined to spoil it by forcing Leslie's
hand. A footing was to be secured upon the opposite
side of the Forth, and a blow threatened upon Perth.
If Leslie attempted to quit his intrenchments to parry
it he was to be attacked in his true front, and compelled
to reoccupy his position. The English army was then to
be thrown suddenly across the Forth, and a dash on Perth
developed before he could move again. Thus the Torwood position would be turned, Stirling taken in reverse,
and no way would remain of loosing Cromwell's new hold
except to attack him on his own ground, or by advancing
into England to compel him to follow. In either case the
victory was almost a certainty for the Commonwealth.

As early as the middle of April part of the flotilla
had arrived, and Monk had made an attack on Burntis-
land. He was repulsed. Cromwell's illness delayed
further operations for some time. At the end of June
he recovered. Major-General Harrison was sent with
all the force that could be spared into Cumberland to
check the expected inroad of the Scots, and Cromwell
advanced to threaten the position at Torwood. Early in
July he moved westward to Glasgow with the double
object of securing the affections of the people in that
quarter and of drawing Leslie's attention away from
the Forth, while the preparations for the descent on the
north bank of the river were completed. On July 17th
a small party landed at North Ferry, rapidly intrenched
themselves, and Lambert followed with a strong division.
Cromwell had moved back to his old position before
Torwood, and as though a direct attack were still his
real object, Monk was ordered to storm an outpost.

All was now ripe, and at the end of July the long
contemplated operation was commenced. In the precision with which it was carried out we may at least see
Monk's unerring hand. The success was complete. By
August 3rd Perth was in the possession of the Commonwealth. Leslie was in full career for the south, and
Cromwell and his generals repassing the Forth in hot
pursuit.

Yet some one must be left behind. The centre
of interest had suddenly shifted, but work in plenty
remained. Some one must be left in the post of peril
to play Cromwell's part while he was gone; some one
who knew how to strike sharp and hard, and could fix
a grip of iron on the country before the army that was

gathering in the Highlands could replace the one that was gone.   Monk was the man, and well he justified the choice.

The force at his command consisted of but four regiments of horse and three of foot, in all less than six thousand men.   With this he attacked Stirling, and on the 16th the maiden castle surrendered.   For this service he received the thanks of Parliament, and was voted £500 a year in Scotch land for ever.

But the work was only commenced.   By the capture of Stirling he had but secured an advanced base from which to operate against the north.   The Committee of Estates, to which Charles had entrusted the kingdom before he left, was sitting at Dundee, and organising, in concert with a number of clan-chieftains, a new army for the King.   Dundee then was Monk's real objective.   No sooner was Stirling in his hands than he hurried forward a small flying column to stop the supplies of the town. Three or four days were spent in disposing of prisoners and booty at Stirling and in setting things in order there, for the most precise strategist of to-day could not be more careful about his base than Monk.   Then the general followed with the bulk of the foot and the siege-train.

Just before reaching Dundee he was joined by a body of cavalry under two officers, who were destined to play a prominent part in history.   The horse were commanded by Colonel Alured, a daring cavalry leader with red-hot political opinions of an advanced socialistic type, an Anabaptist of the Anabaptists.   At the head of the dragoons rode a little fiery man, whom they all adored. It was the famous Colonel Morgan, a soldier of fortune after Monk's own heart, who knew nothing of politics

and everything of his profession. They had probably
served together the greater part of their lives, and were
now at any rate fast friends with unbounded mutual admiration. There was no one to whom Monk would
rather commit a piece of difficult work than this little
dragoon, and he had arrived in the nick of time.

For Monk, as we have seen, with his advanced ideas of
the military art, the Intelligence Department was his
chiefest care. "The eyes of an army," to use his own
expression, he cherished as his own. Spies as usual had
been busy, and now he learned that on his approach the
Government had retired to the Highlands and was sitting
at Alyth, fourteen miles away, at the edge of the hills,
where a force was daily expected to assemble for the relief
of Dundee. Monk at once determined on a surprise so daring that it savours more of romance than the deliberate
expedient of a wary strategist. Morgan was sent for, and
he and Alured were told to take their men, disguised as
far as possible and mixed with Scotch deserters, and
attend the enemy's rendezvous.

Late on the night of the 27th they marched, and unmolested reached Alyth in the first hours of the morning.
To avoid suspicion they boldly marched to the farther side
of the town, and there quietly halted as though they
were a party of the expected troops. No one interfered,
and about three o'clock, after a short rest, when sleep was
the deepest, they suddenly broke into the astonished
town. Hardly a blow was struck. Old Leslie, the commander-in-chief, was taken in his bed, and the rest of
the Government shared his fate; and as Monk went forth
to direct his siege-works Alured and Morgan rode into
camp with three hundred noblemen, lairds, and ministers

prisoners in their train. At one stroke Scotland was as it were beheaded. It was a bloodless victory, as complete almost as the " crowning mercy " at Worcester, now on the eve of being fought. "Truly," wrote Monk in his despatch to Cromwell, "it is a very great mercy which the Lord of Hosts hath been pleased to bestow upon us, observing the time and season. This is the Lord's work, and therefore He alone ought to have the praise." But he concludes by asking for Morgan's promotion. That he could so far have departed from his ordinary style only shows us how great had been the influence of Cromwell's coercive personality upon him.

Still Dundee did not know the extent of the disaster. The garrison could not believe that all hope of relief was at an end, and contemptuously refused Monk's summons. On the third day the batteries opened. All through the last night of August they thundered, and in the morning there was a practicable breach. Monk knew well the garrison was hopelessly demoralised and would be an easy prey, yet he strove to save bloodshed. Twice again he offered them quarter, and twice again they refused. Then at last he gave the word for an assault.

The infantry were very weak from sickness, and the storming parties were strengthened by dismounted troopers and a naval brigade. These elements were not likely to decrease the heat of the fight, and added to this the town was known to contain property of immense value. With incredible fury the breach was carried in one rush. The supports of horse were through almost as soon as the footmen, and a desperate struggle ensued in the streets. In a few minutes it was over and the stormers rushed on wildly through the town hacking

down everything in their way. A number of women, and
even some children who were in the streets, were borne
down in the rush. Soon all that resisted were a party
who with the governor had taken refuge in a tower.
Preparations were being made to smoke them out, when
they asked and received quarter. Unhappily, as the
governor was being taken before Monk he was pistolled
by a fanatic officer, an outrage which the general seems
to have felt as a blot on his own untarnished reputation
as a soldier. Resistance was now at an end, but Monk
seems to have thought it his duty to give over the town
to two days' pillage as a chastisement for its obstinate
refusal of quarter.

The remaining garrisons surrendered on terms in
rapid succession, and the Highland strongholds were one
after another reduced by his officers. He himself took
no active part in the operations. The iron constitution
on which he drew so recklessly during his long campaigns at length gave way, and a few days after the
surrender he was laid up in Dundee with a fever. By
January he had sufficiently shaken it off to be able to
meet the new Scotch commissioners who had arrived
at Dalkeith from London to negotiate the Union, but in
February he was compelled to go south for the benefit
of his health. It is worthy of note that he started on
the journey in the same coach with Lambert, who was
also on the commission, but before Berwick was passed
they agreed to separate, ostensibly because Monk was
too ill to travel fast enough for his rival.

It is said that at this time there was an idea of sending into France ten thousand of those matchless troops
of whom all Europe was talking, as was afterwards done

under Morgan.   For Monk was reserved the superlative honour of commanding them.   But the time was not yet ripe, and instead of figuring as leader of the finest soldiers in the world, for so every one then considered them, Monk went quietly down to Bath to mend his shattered health.

CHAPTER VII

THE waters at Bath completely restored Monk's health, and in July the Council requested Cromwell to order him back to his duty in Scotland, that he might report on the state of the country. Monk did not go.

A new act in the drama had begun. With Dunbar, Worcester, and Monk's successes in Scotland, the Presbyterian party was reduced to impotency. The Independents were triumphant, and the factors of which that party was composed began to detach themselves with ominous distinctness. On the one hand was the Parliament, reactionary in spite of its purging; on the other the army, radical in spite of its leader. For the purpose of understanding Monk's relation to them it is unnecessary to enter minutely into the characteristics of both factions. To place ourselves in sympathy with a political situation it is necessary not so much to understand the aims of the several parties which create it, as to grasp the motives which each party attributes to the other. The great body of politicians are moved more by distrust of their adversaries than by confidence in themselves. Monk at any rate, with his soldierly contempt for politics, was incapable of taking a higher view of the situation

than this. Parliament credited the army with a desire
to establish an arbitrary military government. The army
suspected Parliament of an intention to perpetuate itself
as a tyrannical oligarchy. The latter idea Monk could
endure, the former was for him intolerable. If it came
to a question of army or Parliament, Cromwell knew
that his incorruptible lieutenant would be obstinately
true to his principles and side with the civil power. It
is easy to understand that on the eve of his great stroke
he preferred that his devoted partisan, Major-General
Deane, who was acting in Monk's absence, should continue to command the army in Scotland.

The outbreak of the Dutch war was made an excuse
for keeping the general in England. In view of the
coming struggle it was considered advisable to make
Great Yarmouth a formidable naval port. Monk was
the highest authority on fortification in the service, and
the Council had to consent to his being employed to
carry out the necessary work. In this congenial occupation he remained until November. It was then in contemplation to appoint two admirals to command the
fleet jointly with Blake, according to the usual practice.
Deane, having a considerable naval reputation, was
naturally one, and he was summoned from Scotland,
where Colonel Lilburne, an advanced radical of Anabaptist opinions, succeeded him. Monk was proposed
as the other, but again Cromwell opposed the appointment. He saw the coming crisis almost within measur-
able distance, and naturally wished to see the fleet as
well as the army in the right hands. But this time
his opposition was in vain. On the last day of the
month Blake was defeated by a greatly superior force

under Tromp. The Thames was in danger, and four days later Monk and Deane were ordered to be ready to put to sea in twenty-four hours.

Tromp's victory was, however, too dearly bought for him to pursue Blake, and after his famous cruise in the Channel, as the broom-myth tells, he bore away to Rhé to fetch home the Dutch merchant-fleet that was to assemble there for convoy. All the winter the three generals were busy fitting out a new fleet, and in February they put to sea to intercept Tromp and his costly charge. On the 18th they met, and there ensued one of those extraordinary engagements which distinguished these wars. For three days it lasted, and at the end both sides claimed the victory. Tromp practically saved his huge convoy, while Blake and his partners defeated the Dutch fleet.

Monk's share in the engagements had been comparatively small, as his flagship was a hopelessly slow sailer. Out of his love for heavy artillery he had probably over-gunned it—a common error in the English navy then. At the age of forty-four it is not easy to suddenly take up a new profession, and he made no pretence to seamanship. His complete ignorance of nautical matters became a standing joke. When his ship was coming into action, and the master cried larboard or starboard, Monk used to reply with a cheery shout of "Ay, ay, boys, let us board them!" and he never heard the last of it. When at nightfall on the first day he at length got into action he refused to retire, though his master urgently showed him the danger he ran from fire-ships. "Why," he cried, "the very powder of this ship is enough to blow a fire-ship from it. Charge again!" and away he went through the opposing squadron once more regardless of every protest. Blake had borne the brunt of the action, and had been so severely wounded by an iron splinter that he had to withdraw from active service and leave the command to his two colleagues.

For the next two months Monk was at Portsmouth busily refitting the fleet and crying out continually for supplies and men that would not come, and doing his best to alleviate the sufferings caused by the late battle. No wonder there were vexatious delays when we think what was going on at Whitehall. On April 21st the fleet lay at Spithead all ready for sea except for the delayed stores, when a despatch with strange news was put into the admiral's hands. The blow had fallen : the Revolution was complete : the Rump Parliament was no more. A new Council was sitting at Whitehall, and Cromwell was virtually dictator. What did the fleet mean to do ?

In the quiet dignity of the answer we can see little of Deane's partisanship. Monk's honest indignation glows from between the lines. The whole proceeding was detestable to him ; but staring him in the face was the one thing that ever raised him from his narrow views of duty, and that was the danger of his country. In spite of its insularity there was a genuineness about his patriotism that even won the admiration of his traducers. He made his choice, and took care that the answer which went back should show the reason why. It told in simple language, without a word of approval, how they had very seriously considered the news, and had finally resolved that as the nation had entrusted them with its defence it was their duty to defend it.

In striking contrast was the enthusiastic answer that came back from Lilburne's army in the north. Years afterwards, in a similar crisis, Monk's acquiescence was thrown in his teeth. "I shall answer you that," he wrote. "It was never in my conscience to go out of God's way under the pretence of doing God's work; and you know the variety of times doth much vary the nature of affairs, and what might then patiently be submitted unto, we being engaged with a foreign enemy in a bloody war, cannot be drawn into a precedent at this time after our repentance."

Loyally Monk went on to discharge his country's trust. At the end of April, despairing of their proper equipment, the two generals put to sea and joined Vice-Admiral Penn off Arundel. Together they sailed to the Scotch coast with a fleet of about a hundred sail, and till the end of May cruised in the North Sea from Aberdeen to Yarmouth watching for Tromp and waiting for Blake's squadron to join. On the 30th[1] the Dutch, slightly outnumbering them, were sighted, and three days later, early in the morning, the two fleets met.

Monk and Deane were together on board the *Resolution*, and seem to have attacked line ahead. The wind was light and variable from north-north-west to north-east, and the port division under Lawson, Jordan, and Goodson came into action some time before the rest. The three flagships pierced the line of De Ruyter's division, but as their squadron refused to follow, and Tromp bore down with his whole division to De Ruyter's assistance, for a time they had to engage against over-

[1] Or June 1st. See for this and all the movements at this time Jordan's Log of the *Vanguard*, printed in Penn's *Life of Penn*.

whelming odds. Monk and Deane, seeing the danger,
crowded all sail and plunged into the thick of the fight.
Side by side the two generals stood upon the deck as
they ranged into action. A furious broadside greeted
their approach, and Deane fell at Monk's feet almost cut
in two by a round shot. Horror-stricken the sailors left
their duty to gather round. In a moment Monk had
snatched off his cloak and hidden the shocking sight from
view. Sharply he told the seamen to mind their own
business, and then without moving a muscle of his face
went on fighting his ship as if nothing had happened.
The action, however, did not continue much longer. Wise
as a serpent, though daring as a lion, the father of naval
tactics did not care to fight unless by his skilful manœuvres
he could secure the advantage of numbers, and about
three in the afternoon, when the whole English fleet had
got into action, Tromp drew off.

Monk followed, and at daybreak found himself in
view of the whole Dutch fleet lying off Ostend, but a
dead calm prevailed and he could not move. At sunrise
he signalled all the flag-officers on board the *Resolution*
and announced to them the irreparable loss of yesterday.
By Deane's death the fleet was left in command of a man
who hardly knew one end of a ship from another. But
the old soldier at least could tell how to inspire confidence. He assembled the officers in council of war and
asked for their guidance. "Your advice," he said, "shall
be as binding on me as an Act of Parliament." It was
at once resolved to engage, and that no part of the fleet
might be again isolated by a repetition of yesterday's
faint-heartedness, it was agreed that all the three divi-
sions should attack simultaneously and endeavour to

break up the enemy's line by piercing it in three places.

At noon the wished-for breeze sprang up and a tremendous engagement ensued. The captains who had disgraced themselves, fired by a stirring general order from Monk, vied with the rest to retrieve their reputation, and to such good purpose that the Dutch would not stand by their admiral. In spite of Tromp's signals and angry shots seventy of his ships sailed out of the fight. Thus deserted he was compelled to follow. All day the two fleets stood to the southward close-hauled on a south-westerly breeze, and kept up a hot running fight. About four in the afternoon the wind freshened to a gale, veering to west-south-west, and Monk was able to loose his frigates into the midst of the enemy to reap the harvest of cripples he had put at their mercy. As evening fell Blake's long-expected squadron appeared in the offing, and the Dutch sought refuge towards their own coasts, where at ten o'clock darkness and the shoals stopped further pursuit.

Such was the famous Flanders Battle, the first in which Monk really commanded. The Dutch lost thirty-four ships and for the time were driven from the sea. So well had the English come out of it that without putting in to refit they were able to follow up the victory by a descent upon Cadsand, where a vast quantity of stores were captured or destroyed.

For the next two months, as closely as the weather would allow, the two English admirals blockaded the Dutch coast. Behind their shoals the States were fitting out two fleets. In the Weelings about Flushing was Tromp, at the back of Texel was De Witt; and as Blake was again taken so ill that in July he had to go ashore, on Monk devolved the anxious task of keeping the two consummate Dutch seamen from uniting.

By the end of the month the enemy were ready for sea and Monk was rigorously blockading De Witt at Texel. Early on the 28th a heavy south-westerly gale compelled him to stand out to sea and beat against it all day. At daylight next morning, having recovered sufficient sea-room to be out of danger, he stood away to the south under easy sail, to intercept Tromp whom he expected out. True enough all the previous day the Dutchman had been stealing up the coast to feel for De Witt. About noon on the 29th the two fleets sighted each other. At the same moment the wind shifted to north-north-west and gave Monk the weather-gauge.

Tromp immediately went about. Having lost the wind all he cared to do was to try and draw the English off the Texel. Monk crowded all sail in pursuit, and managed late in the evening to force his enemy into a desultory engagement off Egmont, to which darkness quickly put an end.

All night in thick and heavy weather the chase continued to the southward, but Tromp was too clever for the soldier. In the darkness he doubled back north-north-east, and thus not only recovered the weather-gauge, but in the afternoon managed to join with De Witt, who had slipped out of the Texel as soon as Monk's back was turned.

During the whole of the 30th a tremendous gale was blowing dead on shore. Both fleets attempted to engage, but each time were prevented by the heavy weather. In the morning it cleared. Monk found himself close to

the Dutch coast with the enemy to windward. Unwilling to engage where Tromp would have the advantage
of his knowledge of the shoals, with harbours of refuge
within easy reach, he stood out to sea, and the Dutch
gave chase. They had one hundred and forty sail fresh
from the yards, while Monk had but ninety storm-beaten
ships, with crews sadly thinned and weakened by scurvy,
nor had he a single fire-ship to oppose to those of the
enemy. But dangers could never daunt the general.
As soon as he had recovered sufficient sea-room began
"the most fierce and cruel fight that ever was fought."
It was already the sixth action of the war, and Monk
meant it to be the last. He ordered that no prizes
should be taken or quarter given. "The air," says the
old historian, "was quickly filled with scattered limbs of
men blown up : the sea was dyed with blood."

It was "a very orderly battle" (according to one of
the English flag-officers), in which the old soldier strove
with extraordinary skill to win back the weather-gauge
from the greatest seaman of the day. The two fleets
were standing out to sea, line ahead on parallel courses
and a southerly wind, when the action began by Monk
suddenly tacking on Tromp with the intention of breaking his line. Tromp tacked also to parry the attack, but
though he was clever enough to keep the wind with
nearly the whole of his fleet, a few of his ships were
cut off and put to flight. Then followed three determined encounters, in which each fleet tacked on the
other, passing each time closer and closer in the desperate
struggle for the weather-gauge. Every time Monk dis-
abled some of the Dutch, and every time he pierced
their line and scattered the part he weathered. Still

Tromp kept the advantage with the bulk of his force; but it was at a fearful sacrifice. In the last encounter the ships had fought almost at pike's length. Again and again two of the Dutch admirals had tried to board the *Resolution*, and again and again they had recoiled before the storm of metal that roared from beneath the exultant soldier's feet. Old hands were awestruck at the fury of the fight. "The very heavens," says one, "were obscured with smoke; the air rent with the thundering noise; the sea all in a breach with the shot that fell; the ships even trembling, and we hearing everywhere the messengers of death flying about."

Since sunrise the fight had raged. It was now past two o'clock in the afternoon. Yet again the undaunted soldier of fortune charged; but the Dutch had had their fill. Their splendid fleet had suffered terribly. Tromp's flag had been shot away, and he himself was gasping out his heroic life pierced with a musket ball. Of nine flagships only two were to be seen with the main body. Vice-Admiral Eversen was sinking, and scattered over the waters were burning hulks and the wrecks of captures blown up. As Monk tacked the Dutch spread their crippled wings and ran for Holland. Monk limped after them till evening, burning, sinking, and destroying. Over a hundred sail they had stood out proudly, as the sun rose, in pursuit of the English fleet, "but they were very thin when the sun went down."

As Gravesand steeple rose in sight and the Dutch saw their shoals within reach, Monk gave up the chase. The victory, complete as it was, had not been lightly won, and all that night and the following day his triumphant consorts staggered back to Southwold Bay.

The carnage had been fearful. Eight of Monk's captains lay dead, and eight more were wounded, though he, with his usual luck, had never a scratch. Killed and wounded amounted to over a thousand. The Dutch had lost at least three times as many. Hardly a single English ship was missing. About thirty Dutch were sunk or taken, and barely half the fleet were together at the last.[1]

The war was practically at an end. Though the intrepid Dutch were soon as busy refitting as Monk himself, every one knew a decisive action had been fought. A public thanksgiving was ordered, and honours were showered on Monk and poor Blake and their officers. Next to Cromwell the soldier of fortune was now the greatest man in the land. Yet, in spite of his greatness, and in spite of the ardour with which he threw himself into the work of refitting the fleet, he found time and conscience to do a little act of humble duty before he put to sea again.

In the midst of the shouts of triumph was a voice that he loved, perhaps, as well as all his golden chains and medals, whispering that a child was to be born to him, and born in sin. Ratsford was dead. So quietly in the midst of his pressing work he snatched an hour to repair as far as could be the wrong he had done. Like an honest man, he took the perfumer's widow to St. George's Church in Southwark, and there he made her his wife.

During the remainder of this year and the beginning

[1] For the whole battle *cf.* the published despatches with the principal flag-officer's account, Gumble's *Life*, p. 67 ; Vice-Adm. Jordan's Log and Hoste's account, both printed in Penn's *Life of Penn ;* and the three despatches in *Cal. S. P. Dom.*, August 2nd.

of the next Monk was busily engaged in maintaining
the blockade of the Dutch coast, and attending to the
routine business of his place at Whitehall and Chatham.
Indeed he had little time for anything else. In June,
while he was in search of Tromp's fleet, he had been
called by the Protector to the Little Parliament, but his
legislative duties sat lightly upon him. No doubt he
was reconciled to the new form of government by the
express declaration of the Council, which almost seems
to have been put in for his especial benefit, that the
sword ought to have no share in the civil power. Still
he appears to have attended the sittings but seldom.
Once only are we sure he was there, and that was to
receive the thanks of Parliament. His visionary
colleagues were for him contemptible. The war and
his magnificent new flag-ship, the *Swiftsure*, were
much more to his mind, and he can only have rejoiced
when he saw the power of Parliament suddenly surrendered into Cromwell's hands.

The new rule had his entire approval. A single
person, as we have seen, was his ideal of government,
and especially when that single person was one well
able to apply the "principal and able remedy against
civil wars." The crisis had resolved itself into a situation after his own heart. In the despotic Protector he
saw a warlike prince; in the Dutch war a physic for
him to minister to his country's disease. But he was
doomed to disappointment. The Protector's statecraft
was less crude than his lieutenant's, and in spite of
Monk's energetic and even angry protests peace on comparatively easy terms was signed with Holland on April
5th, 1654.

CHAPTER VIII

CROMWELL had now other work for his most trusted officer. General Middleton had landed in Scotland to fan the flame which Lord Glencairn had kindled for the King, and which Morgan had nearly smothered. The Highlands were in a blaze, the Lowlands were seething in the heat, and Lilburne showed himself incapable of coping with the growing danger in spite of the fiery little dragoon's assistance.

Since February the rising had been getting every day more serious, and still no one was sent to supersede Lilburne. Cromwell at the outset of his reign felt the Scotch command was the most critical appointment he had to make. Not only was Scotland the chief field of Royalist action, but the Parliamentary army there was ultra-Independent, and sullenly disgusted to see a monarchy practically re-established. A man must go who could crush the Royalists speedily, and, which was still more important, who could be trusted with a victorious army of Irreconcilables afterwards. There was absolutely no one who fulfilled the conditions but Monk. In December it had been settled that he was to go, but till the Dutch war was over he could not be spared by the

Admiralty.   Day by day the news from the north grew
worse, and still the Dutch struggled in Cromwell's grip
to avoid the article for the seclusion of the Stuarts.   At
last it was done, and on April 6th, the very day after
the treaty was signed, Monk got his route for Scotland
with the fullest powers.

A fortnight later he reached Dalkeith, and at once
threw himself into the preliminary organisation of that
forgotten campaign in which, if ever, the Highlands were
for the first time conquered.

It is a campaign of the highest interest, and well re-
pays the laborious task of piecing it together from the
obscure and confused notices that are extant.   Hitherto
Highland warfare had been little more than aimless hunts
after an ever-shifting and disappearing objective.   For
the first time the rules of modern strategy were to be
applied to it.   The latest model for mountain warfare
was the Duc de Rohan's brilliant Valtelline campaign of
1635.   It was the admiration of all Europe, and has even
been considered worthy of a commentary by the Arch-
duke Charles himself.   Two such professed soldiers as
Monk and Middleton must have been perfectly familiar
with it.   Monk at least had studied the duke's *Perfect
Captaine* with an enthusiasm which his own *Observations*
too plainly betrays ; and the scientific way in which he
now went to work shows that he either invented or had
learnt a thoroughly digested system.

His general idea was to cut the Highlands asunder
along the line of what is now the Caledonian Canal, and
to fix his enemy within one of two definite areas, where
he could operate against him as he chose.   The area to
the north of the line was sufficiently determined by its

geographical conformation, but that to the south had to be firmly marked by strategical positions. Already a chain of fortresses and strong posts stretching from Inverness through Stirling to Ayr shut it in on the south and east, and during the next two months, while Monk was waiting for the grass to grow sufficiently for him to be able to move his cavalry, the investment was completed. On the west, from Glencoe to the head of Loch Lomond, diplomacy secured Argyle's country in a state of armed neutrality, and at each of the four salient angles of the area was established an independent base. One was at Inverness, one at Perth, and a third at Kilsyth, between Stirling and Glasgow, with Leith for its supporting base. The fourth by a bold stroke was to be planted in the heart of the enemy's country at Lochaber, with supporting bases at Liverpool and Ayr, whereby he would complete his quadrilateral and secure the southern end of his dividing line. From these points he intended to act on double lines of operation, with two strong columns keeping light touch with one another, and each able at any moment to act in a new direction by a rapid change of base. One of them he was to lead himself, while Morgan took command of the other. Their organisation was a source of the greatest care. As he was not likely to meet horse in any numbers, Monk boldly eliminated from the foot nearly the whole of the pikes on which the steadiness of infantry was supposed to depend, and filled his ranks almost entirely with musketeers.

To the labour of laying this elaborate foundation for the campaign was added the task of reducing the army to some sense of discipline. Monk had found it badly demoralised by the incapacity of Lilburne, and the

H

license which he had allowed to religious controversy. On all this he set his foot, and at the same time endeavoured to repair the mischief which the wanton insolence of the sectaries had done, by inaugurating a conciliatory policy towards the Scots—a policy, however, which he was careful to fortify by a system of strong patrols in the Lowlands.

At present there was no need to press offensive operations. Middleton was still in Sutherland, and from Dingwall Morgan was watching him, ready to fall on him if he attempted to join the Lochaber chiefs. In the middle of May Monk moved to Stirling to see that all the outlets from the hills were sufficiently secured to prevent forays in that direction. Having ordered the construction of redoubts and the staking of fords wherever necessary, he joined the first column at Kilsyth in order to more deeply mark the south-west limit of his southern area by operations in the Ben Lomond hills. First, however, an important step was taken. A column, consisting of two thousand men and furnished with all necessary materials for establishing the fourth base, was being secretly organised in Ireland to seize Inverlochy. The time was now ripe for the attempt, and Colonel Brayne was despatched to bring it over. This done, Monk commenced his work. The difficulties of the undertaking at once declared themselves. The moment he moved, Glencairn, who occupied the Ben Lomond country, began raiding in his rear and stopped him. But the veteran of the Irish wars had learnt when to be bold, and without hesitation he flew at his enemy's throat. Advancing resolutely over the Kilsyth hills and up the headwaters of the Forth into the heart of

the Ben Lomond range, he compelled Glencairn to concentrate and occupy a strong position at Aberfoyle.
Here Monk attacked him.   Again and again he was repulsed.   But the discipline of the "red soldier" told at
last, and Glencairn had to give way.   The hills were
cleared, every boat on the loch destroyed, and the
western boundary of the southern area completed with
an impassable stretch of water from Argyle's country
to the banks of the Clyde.

Meanwhile Middleton had outwitted Morgan.   Breaking up his force he had slipped it piecemeal over the
hills and had joined his friends in Lochaber.   It was
the signal for active operations.   Leaving a small force
to cover Glasgow, and ordering up the Border horse
under Colonel Howard in support, Monk suddenly
shifted on to the Perth line and plunged into the hills.
He meant if possible to drive the enemy through the
gap he had left into the Lowlands, where they would fall
an easy prey to his horse, or, if that failed, to force them
northward.   Moving with startling rapidity he was
soon entangled in the wildest of the enemy's mountains
and morasses.   It was a country which till Deane's
demonstration two years ago had been considered in-
accessible to Lowland troops.   It swarmed with roving
bands of Highlanders; every straggler was a doomed
man; the horse could hardly move, and the whole
work of the march was arduous beyond all experience.
But bold as was Monk's project its execution was
cautious in the extreme.   Every step of the way he
made good.   The country was systematically ravaged
and every castle of strategic importance captured, gar-
risoned, and turned into an advanced magazine, according

to the somewhat cumbrous and pedantic system which
Monk and his contemporaries were then introducing.
To prevent surprise and give time for properly securing
his quarters he never marched after mid-day, nor did he
ever move without flanking parties and a cloud of scouts.
He marked out each camp and placed every picket and
sentry himself, and was, in short, the head and heart
alike of his over-worked force.

Indifferent to hunger and sleep himself, he took every
care of his men. He doctored and dosed them with his
own hand, and by his elaborate system of magazines
he kept them well supplied with biscuits and cheese.
At the same time he took care his officers should not
grumble. When the day's work was done it was his
wont to unbend in frankest good fellowship. Then while
his canteen was unpacked it was his delight to sit on
the grass beside it and pitch joints of cold meat to his
officers, who gathered round. No one could bear the
hardships of a campaign better than tough "old George,"
and no one knew better how to lighten them.

No wonder the work prospered. On June 9th
Monk had started, and by the 11th he had established
his first advanced magazine at the foot of Loch Tay.
Here he received intelligence from Morgan, who was
operating from Inverness on the line of the Spey, that
Middleton had summoned a rendezvous of the clans at
Loch Ness head, anticipating a move from the south.
Monk at once turned northward and ordered Morgan
on to the line of the lochs, with instructions to close in
behind Middleton as soon as he passed over it. Brayne,
he knew, had left Ireland a week ago, and between the
three columns he felt sure of forcing the Royalists into

an engagement. The zeal of the impetuous Morgan
spoiled the combination. So rapidly did he move that
he fell in with the Royalist vanguard as it emerged
from Glengarry and flung it violently back into the
hills. The result was that as Monk descended the
northern slopes of the Grampians Middleton retreated
to Kintail. Still much had been gained. The surprise
from Ireland had proved a complete success, and right
and left Monk was now able to join hands with Morgan
and Brayne along the line of the lochs. Middleton
and his friends were thus shut within the northern area,
where Monk could renew his combined operations on
definite lines. Loch Ness head was now in touch with
Inverness by means of a gunboat which had been
dragged up into the dock. Here Morgan was established,
while the general advanced up Glen Moriston to try
and drive his enemy northward or into his lieutenant's
arms. In the effort Monk fairly surpassed himself.
The country proved more difficult every step he took:
the weather was so violent that the cattle could not
keep the hills; yet from glen to glen Monk and his
red column chased Middleton and his Highland chivalry.
Such marching astounded them. At every stride the
Southron trod on their heels, and twice they had to
abandon stores in order to keep out of his reach. But
flesh and blood could not stand such work for long, and
at the end of a week Monk retired to reprovision from
Inverness, having laid waste the whole of the country
from which Middleton was drawing his supplies, and set
the "red cock crowing" in the home of every chief who
had joined him.

Still Middleton had won the round. He had avoided

an action, and but for the new scheme of which his head was full Monk was as far from his end as ever. His new idea was to send Morgan by sea to destroy the Royalist winter-quarters in Caithness, while he himself covered Inverness. It was a stroke which Middleton would clearly be compelled to parry by an offensive movement to the south or a march into Caithness. Either would suit Monk's disposition, and Morgan prepared to embark. The effect was immediate. Two days later Middleton was seen by the garrison at Blair Athol, and in two more Morgan was lying in wait at Braemar and Monk in hot pursuit over the Grampians on the Royalist track. Through the Drumouchter Pass and Badenoch his recruited column swept, and on into Athol, ravaging as it went, till Athol was as black and desert as Lochaber and Kintail. From Breadalbane the chase turned westward, and now so close did Monk dog the enemy's steps that not a levy could be held, and their forces began rapidly to shrink from exhaustion.

From Loch Tay through Glen Dochart, from Glen Lochy through Strathfillan, the pursuit continued to the head of Loch Awe. The Cavalier chiefs were resolved to force Argyle to take one side or the other, and here they had caught him in Glenorchy's castle. But the siege was not two days old when Monk was upon them and raised it. Foiled in their great scheme on Argyle they doubled back into Perthshire, but still there was no rest. While he ravaged Glenorchy and Glenstrea Monk detached a brigade to keep them moving, and Middleton began to see the end was near. What his enemy's activity left undone the wrangling of his friends was completing, and harassed past bearing with their

bickerings and jealousies, he resolved to return to the
north. Monk knew his intention, as he knew everything; and Morgan was rapidly shifted to the headwaters
of the Spey, with orders to feel his way through Badenoch and the Drumouchter Pass on the look-out for
Middleton, towards Loch Rannoch, while down Glen
Lyon the general pushed him blindly to his fate. To
avoid him, as Monk expected, Middleton struggled over
the hills into Glen Rannoch, and thence, persuaded by
false intelligence that the two English generals were
together, made a rapid move up the Perthshire Glengarry for the Drumouchter Pass. Beside the little Loch
at its foot was a hamlet, where he intended to halt for
the night. Weary and half starved his vanguard reached
the spot towards evening, but only to be received with a
volley from Morgan's pickets. Descending the pass that
very day on his way to Glen Rannoch, the little dragoon
had occupied the identical quarters Middleton had intended for himself. The surprise was complete. Morgan
was expecting Middleton, though not quite so soon.
Middleton was only looking behind him where he believed
Morgan to be with Monk. The smart dragoon, always
prepared for anything, immediately hurled his fresh and
well-armed troops upon the weary Scots as they lay helpless between the Loch and the hills, and scattered them to
the four winds.

To rally them in the face of Monk's forces proved
impossible. Middleton fled to Caithness, whither Morgan
pursued him, while Monk occupied himself with Athol
and Glencairn. Driving them before him towards the
trap he had so cleverly prepared in the Ben Lomond
hills, he compelled them to disband and leave him to

complete his work. Then one after another he destroyed their winter-quarters in the remote fastnesses
about the loch which Rob Roy was to make so famous,
and which had been hitherto considered entirely in-
accessible to Southrons. By the end of August the
work was done, and the general was able to return
to Dalkeith. The back of the insurrection was broken.
The Highlands were bound in chains of fortified posts.
The garrisons gave those who stirred not a moment's
peace. Unable to combine, unable even to feed their
followers, one after another the chiefs came in, till at
last the Highlands were so quiet that there was hardly
a man left with heart to lift a cow, and he who would
find a stray, it used to be said, need only send a crier
round.

To enter into the details of Monk's subsequent
administration is impossible here. Indeed it hardly
belongs to his career as a man of action. The art of
governing a conquered country he had always held to be
part of a soldier's education, and he now applied to his
province the principles which he had long ago laid
down during his solitude in the Tower. The most
important thing he considered to assure the conquest of
a free people was to take away the desire of revolting,
"and to do this," he wrote, "you must not take away
their hopes of recovering their liberties by their good
obedience, . . . and therefore you must always begin
in a fair way." And well he did it. On easy terms the
chiefs were admitted to make their peace, and security
for good behaviour was taken from them. Every
facility was afforded them of entering foreign services,
and those who remained at home were disarmed.

" Assist the weak inhabitants," he said, " and weaken the
mighty." Never perhaps in the history of Scotland
had the weak been so strong. They began to look
on the soldiers under Monk's strict discipline as
the best friends they had. The feuds and brigandage
which had so long distracted the country became entirely
unknown. Trade began to revive : taxes came in
plentifully ; and Monk began to lay the foundation
of the rich public treasure without which he considered
no Government was safe.

There being a difficulty about engaging the people in
a foreign war, Monk encouraged the Cavalier chiefs
to raise troops for service as mercenaries abroad. But
the King was shrewd enough to privately forbid it, and
Monk had to fall back upon his other rules for the
prevention of civil strife. The first was the perfection
of the fortresses, the other the attainment so far as
possible of uniformity of religion. The restrictions
which Lilburne had placed upon the Presbyterians
were gradually removed, and the Kirkmen encouraged
at the expense of the sectaries. But while he gave
them complete religious freedom, he was careful to strip
the clergy of all temporal power by forbidding them
the use of excommunication and by suspending the
assemblies of the Kirk.

From Dalkeith Monk governed the country in peace,
attending to almost every detail himself. At first it is
true that occasional plots disturbed his serenity, but his
method of dealing with conspirators was as successful as it was original. It is, moreover, replete with
a grim humour which gives us a new insight into his
character. Such chiefs as fell under suspicion were

arrested and placed under rigorous confinement. In noisome dungeons they were visited by Monk's roughest officers, and sometimes by the terrible general himself. There they were urged to confess, and even threatened with the torture. Those who yielded were at once released with a caution and never troubled again. Those who held out firmly were asked to dinner at Dalkeith, where the sound sense and excellent claret of their good-natured host soon brought them to reason. By this happy treatment the shrewd general found out at once whom he could safely ignore and who were dangerous. The first he knew he had frightened into good behaviour ; of the others he made friends.

Most notable of these was young Cameron of Lochiel, the Ulysses of the Highlands, the wolf-slayer, the man who had saved his life by tearing out the throat of one of Brayne's soldiers with his teeth. Evan Dhu was, in fact, the ideal hero of the clansmen, and though his action had been paralysed by the Inverlochy garrison, he had been the most dangerous and indefatigable figure in the late rising. He had been almost the last to come in, but from the day of his surrender the idol of the clans became Monk's devoted personal friend. These two men, so utterly different and yet in much so alike, seem to have conceived for each other an unbounded admiration. Monk gave the Prince of Robbers, as Charles the Second used to call him, a share in the administration of Lochaber, and supported him in his law-feuds, while at the crisis of Monk's career Lochiel attached himself to his staff and rode with him to London.

There was but one event which seriously broke the harmony of the tranquil life at Dalkeith, and that was

the widespread Republican conspiracy of 1654. As
Cromwell's most trusted officer Monk was one of its
principal objects. In Morgan's absence the appointment
of major-general on the governor's staff was held by
Milton's friend, sweet-mannered Colonel Overton. The
general shared the poet's high opinion of his honour,
and had persuaded the Protector that his politics,
radical as they were, would never make him forget his
duty. This man accepted the management of the plot
in Scotland. The idea was to assassinate Monk, seize
the Government, and march with the Scotch army to
the support of the English Republicans. To this end
the army was widely tampered with, and as a matter of
course the proceedings of the conspirators came to the
vigilant general's ears. Quietly he allowed the plot to
mature as if he suspected nothing, and then on the eve
of its execution suddenly changed his guards, pounced
upon the conspirators, and sent them all up to London
under arrest.

"I am convinced," he wrote to Cromwell in for-
warding some papers of Overton's which he had
subsequently discovered, "if your Highness do but
weigh the letters well, you will find Colonel Overton
had a design to promote the Scots king's business."
Whatever was the part which the Cavaliers played in
the plot, these letters certainly contain no evidence of
their complicity. But Monk would believe anything of
a soldier who had been false to his colours, and his
comment is amusingly characteristic. It would seem
that he had so little troubled himself with politics as to
have entirely failed to grasp the situation. At this
time he had probably got little beyond the original

question of Parliament and King.   Of the endless
factions into which his own party was splitting he
appears to have had but little understanding, except in
so far as they led to insubordination in the army.
Against a Royalist enemy he had been sent to Scotland,
and he saw a Royalist enemy at the bottom of every
trouble.

Indeed it was at this time that he seems to have been
first getting into that nervous and irritable state with
regard to the King and his affairs from which he was
never safe till Charles was on his throne.   He was
perfectly contented where he was.   As the military
governor of a conquered kingdom, he had reached the
highest ambition of a soldier of fortune.   He was now
getting on for fifty, and desired nothing so much as
to quietly enjoy his position with his wife and children,
to whom he was devoted.   Indeed, the death of George,
the baby, about this time seems to have upset him more
than all the difficulties of his office together.   But his
friends would not leave him in peace.

Eager to propitiate the Scots, he kept open house at
Dalkeith, and through the influence of the Countess of
Buccleuch the nobility began to accept his hospitality.
They soon came to have a liking for the kindly general.
He received them indeed so cordially, and seemed so
anxious to be on good terms with them, that there is no
doubt some of them began to see in the simple-minded
soldier a possible instrument for the revival of their
party.   Early in November, 1655, he had intercepted two
autograph letters from the king, one addressed to " 2,"
whom he knew to be Lord Glencairn ; the other to " T,"
a cypher he did not understand.   The letter, however,

was of a highly compromising nature. " T " was told that the King was assured of his affection, and he was encouraged to be ready when the time was ripe. According to his usual practice Monk took copies of both the letters and allowed them to proceed to their destination. The copies he forwarded at once to Cromwell, assuring him that he would soon know to whom the " T " letter was delivered, and be able to deal with him as he deserved. To his intense annoyance it was delivered to himself. Cromwell seems to have thoroughly enjoyed the joke, but Monk was furious, and vented his anger by arresting Glencairn, whom he evidently suspected of being at the bottom of it.

Yet in spite of all he could do the Cavaliers chose to believe that he was a king's man at heart, and to make him the object of their intrigues. His uneasiness was increased by his new chaplain Price, who, having obtained considerable influence over Mrs. Monk, set her on to advocate the martyr's cause. It must be confessed that the general was a little henpecked at home, and a little afraid of his wife's sharp tongue ; so, like a wise man, he let her talk treason to her heart's content without reply, and told Price whenever the subject was mentioned that he had no sympathy with the cause of a man who had shown himself hopelessly incapable of governing. If the martyr had been fit to reign, he used to say, he would have taken his advice and fought the Scots in 1638.

Still they all pretended not to believe him, and his nervousness became chronic. Cromwell was only amused at his distress. He never forgot the letter to " T." The joke appealed to the Protector's peculiar sense of humour. Nearly three years later, when Monk one day returned

to Dalkeith, he found a letter had been mysteriously left
with the guard. It proved apparently to be one of the
same tenor as the first, and more furious than ever he
sent a copy of it up to the Secretary of State. "I did
not think fit to trouble his Highness with it," the general
wrote, "it being, as I conceive it is, a knavish trick of
some Scotchman or other. . . . I hope God will enable
me as I make them smart for this roguery and the former
report which they made of me." Of course Thurloe told
Cromwell, and the Protector could not resist adding his
well-known "drolling" postscript to his next despatch.
"There be some that tell me," he wrote to Monk shortly
before his death, "that there is a certain cunning fellow
in Scotland called George Monk who is said to lie in wait
there to introduce Charles Stuart; I pray you use your
diligence to apprehend him and send him up to me."
Clearly he was poking fun at his lieutenant. The Protector knew well enough he was to be trusted implicitly.
He sent him up all his most disaffected troops, knowing
that under Monk's stern discipline they would soon be
brought to their senses. He gave him full powers to
cashier any officer he liked. He abandoned his intention
of reducing the army when Monk said it was not safe.
He even left him nearly two years without a Council to
watch him, and only restored it upon Monk's urgent and
repeated entreaties for help in his work.

As part of their intrigues the Cavaliers industriously
spread reports that Cromwell was afraid of his lieutenant.
They said the Protector tried to get him out of Scotland
by offering him the command of the great Jamaica
expedition, and that Monk, seeing through his designs,
refused. As a matter of fact Cromwell did want to see

his darling project conducted by the most able and experienced commander in his service, but reluctantly abandoned the idea in consequence of a confidential report that Scotland would not be safe out of Monk's hands. So the post was not offered him. If it had been he would certainly have accepted it. To lead such an enterprise was the dream of Monk's life. The rumour was revived in 1658 because the general did not attend Cromwell's "other House," to which he had been called. It was said that he had refused the summons, but it was untrue. The real explanation of his absence is that there were at the time signs of a Royalist descent, and he told the Protector he dared not come till some one was appointed to take his place. No one was appointed, and he remained.

In fact he was an ideal governor. Everything seemed to go smoothly, and he never bothered except now and then for money that was due. In spite of the endless questions that must have arisen every day, half his letters to the Secretary of State at this period contain apologies for having no news. A great part of the rest consist of information on purely English affairs. The hard-worked and anxious Protector knew well how priceless is such a governor, and could laugh securely at what the Cavaliers said when he knew what a bugbear to his trusty friend were Charles Stuart and all his works.

But while Cromwell laughed and Monk fumed at the Cavalier tricks we must cast a glance down into Devonshire, where a web more subtle and secret than any that had yet been tried was being spun to catch the incorruptible proconsul. Almost at the end of the world, in his rectory at Plymtree, sat Nicholas Monk. There all through those dangerous and unquiet times he had "possessed a sweet and comfortable privacy" after his own heart. To-day a messenger disturbed him at his books. It was a letter from cousin John asking him to come and see him. Sir John Grenville was the son of Sir Bevil by Elizabeth Monk, and nephew to George's old friend Sir Richard. He was a great man now, and an active figure in Lord Mordaunt's new group of ardent young Cavaliers who were trying to goad the old Royalists of the "Sealed Knot" out of the lethargy to which they had been reduced by fines and failures and distrust of the King and each other. A little flurried, we may be sure, the quiet parson hurried away, but found with relief it was no business of state. Only Sir John had a fat living fallen vacant, and he thought cousin Nicholas might like it. He wanted nothing for it either, only if he *should* ever happen to have any business with cousin George up in Scotland perhaps Nicholas would not mind making himself useful. Certainly he would not; so in due course he finds himself in clover at his new living of Kelkhampton, and a distinct step is taken to the Restoration.

As yet Grenville knew it was useless to approach his cousin. He had taken the Protector's commission and had promised Cromwell, it was said, to support his dynasty. So when Oliver died in September, 1658, Richard was duly proclaimed at Edinburgh; but in spite of Monk's efforts it was without a note of enthusiasm. The soldiers grumbled when the ceremony was over that they had to support a man they did not know. "Old George for my money," said one with applause; "he is fitter for a Protector than Dick Cromwell!" No doubt

Oliver thought so too. He had told Richard always to follow Monk's advice; and one of the new Protector's first acts was to send Dr. Clarges, Monk's brother-in-law, and now Commissary-General for the Irish and Scotch armies, on a special mission to Scotland, to seek the advice and support of his father's right-hand man.

It was excellent advice that Clarges brought back. True to his simple creed, Monk told Richard he must break the political power of the army and gather round him to share in the government the natural leaders of the people. He showed him exactly how to do it, but Richard was too weak or too indolent to follow his instructions. His only idea was to offer Monk a large sum of money to support him by force. Dearly as he loved riches, Monk refused. He had pledged himself to the Cromwells, and that was enough. Richard would want all his money himself. Every day the Republican army, with Lambert and Fleetwood at its head, grew stronger, and the "new Royalists," as they called the Cromwellians, grew weaker. Before he had been eight months on the throne Richard gave up the struggle, dissolved his Parliament, and weakly identified himself with the army. The inevitable result followed. At the end of May he abdicated in favour of a military republic.

The leading officers formed themselves into a provisional government, and took immediate steps to recall the Republican remnant of the Long Parliament, which since its expulsion by Cromwell had come to be looked upon as representing the "good old cause" of the Commonwealth. It was at all events a pretence of constitutionalism, and Monk seized the excuse to sullenly acquiesce in the new order. "Had Richard not dis-

solved his Parliament," he always said, "I would have
marched down to support it," and in view of his subsequent conduct there is every reason to believe he meant
what he said. But Richard had pusillanimously thrown
up the game before his friend could help him, and Monk
was not a man to plunge his country into civil war in
such a hopeless cause. And so when his kinsman Cornet
Monk arrived from Ireland on a special mission from
Henry Cromwell he found he was too late.

The first act of the restored "Rump" was one of the
last importance. In their eagerness to get control over
the army they insisted on every officer receiving his commission from themselves at the hands of the Speaker.
Monk accepted a new commission with the rest, and from
that moment he was as devoted a servant to Parliament
as ever he had been to Cromwell; but, unlike Cromwell,
the new Government committed the folly of not trusting
him. The Council of State immediately set to work to
fill his army with their own nominees. Monk protested,
and refused to permit the new men to act without the
Speaker's commission. Fortunately public business was
so disturbed in London that most of these commissions
never arrived.

To the Government's distrust Monk replied with contempt. His despatches at this time are curt and peremptory. He obviously detested the new state of things,
and acquiesced in it only because it staved off the evil
day he dreaded when he would be dragged, sword in hand,
into the miserable political struggle which he had hitherto so successfully avoided. He sullenly did his duty, and
that was all. He informed the Government of Royalist
movements as regularly as ever, and engaged as actively

in keeping the country quiet.   Still, as though he foresaw
the need his country was soon to have for Scotland's
goodwill, he began to relax his hold, and with complete
success.   " The last two years of his government," it was
said by a Scotchman, "were so mild and moderate, except
with respect to the clergy, whose petulant and licentious
tongues he curbed upon all occasions, that the nation would
not have willingly changed it for any other but that of
their natural prince."   Yet his rule was so complete
that in Scotland the great Royalist plot that was now
in full maturity could not even show its head.

CHAPTER IX

THE ABORTIVE PRONUNCIAMENTO

MONK was now on the eve of the remarkable adventure which was to lift him from the position of an able officer to the dignity of a great historical figure. Fifty was then considered a ripe old age, and while most men of his years were looking round for a resting-place, he was about to begin his political career.

It was none of his own seeking. Thrifty and business-like to a fault, he had amassed a considerable fortune, and he began to turn his eyes longingly to his property in Ireland. At Ballymurn, between Wexford and Enniscorthy, he had an estate which had been granted to him in satisfaction of arrears of pay. It was in the midst of the most fertile and prosperous part of the island, and within easy reach of his old home. Ever since the beginning of 1657, with the colonial instinct still strong within him, he had been writing to Henry Cromwell, the Lord-Deputy of Ireland, that his only ambition now was to settle down as an Irish planter. All that kept him at his post, he told him, was his desire to see "your father and my dear friend better settled in his affairs." With Oliver's death and Richard's fall that motive was gone. Since Lambert had reappeared upon the scene his rela-

tions with head-quarters had not been pleasant. Each
day they grew more strained, and he longed for retire-
ment more ardently than ever.

Apart from politics his life at Dalkeith was pleasant
enough. In the short intervals of relaxation from business he devoted himself to planting, gardening, and hunt-
ing, of which he was passionately fond. He was a man
of strong domestic affections, and they grew with advancing years. On the whole his family life was happy.
His wife was possessed of many good qualities. She
was devoted to him, and in spite of her sharp tongue
he was very fond of her. The loss of his baby son
George was a great and lasting grief, but Christopher,
his first-born, was left. Daughters he had none, but
Mary Monk, the eldest girl of his favourite brother,
had come to stay with him, and even now he was in
correspondence with her father about her marriage and
the dowry he was going to provide.

But however attractive grew the prospect of a quiet
life in Ireland far away from the din of politics, retire-
ment was now out of the question. On July 5th, 1659,
he found it his duty to write the following warning to
the Council of State: "I make bold to acquaint you
that I hear that Charles Stuart hath laid a great design
both in England and Ireland, but as yet I hear nothing
that he hath written over to this country concerning
that business. I am confident that if he had I should
have heard of it."

By a strange irony almost as he penned the words
his cousin, Sir John Grenville, was in consultation with
Lord Mordaunt as to the best method of making the
general a party to their design. It was the wide-

spread conspiracy for a simultaneous rising of the
King's friends in every county of which the vigilant
governor had heard. Fortified with a new commission
from the King, Mordaunt and his beautiful and coura-
geous young wife had succeeded in hatching a really fine
plot in concert with the more energetic members of the
Sealed Knot. King and Cavaliers were to be kept
in the background, and those constitutional Royalists,
who as far as possible had never been in arms for the
Crown, were to rise for a free Parliament and "the
known laws of the land."

Mordaunt, in spite of his youth and the ardent enthusiasm which had goaded the inert Knot into taking
up the movement, had a clear head. In his heart he
knew that much more was to be done by gaining the
leaders of the Opposition than by the best planned risings,
and for him Monk's adhesion, or at least his neutrality,
was of the first importance. By the whole of the King's
councillors, however, the general, to his honour, was
looked upon as unapproachable. It was in this difficulty
that his sanguine young cousin saw the opportunity for
which he had been so long preparing, and declared himself ready to undertake the task. At his request he
was armed with an effusive letter from Charles to
Monk, and a commission leaving him free to treat, with
the sole limit that no more than a hundred thousand
pounds a year was to be promised to the general and his
officers. Grenville lost not a moment, and a few days
later poor book-loving Nicholas was startled in his quiet
Cornish rectory by a peremptory summons to London.

Monk's warning was not the only one which reached
the Council. Sir Richard Willis, the most trusted

member of the Knot and an old friend of Monk's, was
revealing everything but the names of the Cavaliers
engaged. The only anxiety of the Government was to
conceal its information from the conspirators. At every
point it was ready. Lambert and Fleetwood were old
hands at the work. Their idea apparently was to allow
the rising to take place, tempt the King to land, and
then inflict a blow which would at once crush their adversaries and give themselves an unassailable prestige.
Amongst other precautions Monk was ordered to send
two regiments of horse and two of foot into England,
and it is significant that he obeyed without demur.

At the last moment an officious postmaster spoilt all.
In a fit of zeal he intercepted an important letter. The
Royalists got to hear of it, lost their heads, and the
rising was nipped in the bud, or abandoned everywhere
but in Cheshire and Lancashire. There Sir George
Booth successfully established himself, and Lambert
marched against him.

Amidst the din and bustle of military preparation
Nicholas Monk arrived in London, and with no little
alarm heard from Grenville's lips what was required
of him. Ostensibly for the purpose of settling his
daughter's marriage, and bringing her back to Cornwall,
he was to carry the King's letters to his brother and
negotiate the secret treaty. Nicholas flatly refused to
touch the letters. They were far too dangerous. He
consented, however, to carry a verbal message, and was
solemnly sworn not to breathe a word of the very
delicate affair to any one but his brother.

The only difficulty was how to reach Dalkeith.
Lambert's troops blocked every road, and it was found

necessary to take Clarges into their confidence. The
only objection was that the cunning commissary, who
knew everything, would certainly not believe Nicholas
was going on his daughter's account. He had to be told
that the parson's real mission was from the constitutional
gentry of Devon and Cornwall. Some such mission he
really had. Clarges refused to engage in the affair, but
consented to provide Nicholas with a passage on a
Government ship to Leith, and cautioned him against
letting any one know his business except Dr. Barrow,
the general's physician, and Dr. Price, his private
chaplain.

Meanwhile Monk was being approached from another
quarter. Lord Fairfax, it is said, had undertaken as
part of the general movement to raise the gentlemen
of the north, but he was far too good a soldier not
to see the futility of the attempt if Monk chose to
oppose it. He would not stir till he had come to an
understanding with the Scots' governor, and to this end
Colonel Atkins, on pretence of visiting relations in Fife,
was ordered to go to Dalkeith. Atkins had commanded a company under Monk in Lord Leicester's
regiment in 1641. They were old brothers-in-arms, and
Monk received him so kindly that the colonel ventured
to disclose the intention of the gentlemen of the north,
and ask the general what he would do if they began
to make their levies. He had his answer in a moment.
"If they do appear," said Monk sharply, "I will send a
force to suppress them. By the duty of my place I can
do no less."

Such was his reply, but "the duty of my place" was
for him no longer the magic solvent of all ethical diffi-

culties that it had been.   During his long proconsulship
" honest George " had developed from the soldier into the
statesman.   True he clung still to his cherished first-born
as ardently as ever.   " I am not one of those," he had just
written to the Speaker, " that seek great things, having
had my education in a commonwealth where soldiers
received and observed commands but gave none. . . .
Obedience is my great principle, and I have always and
ever shall reverence the Parliament's resolution in civil
things as infallible and sacred."   That the military power
must be subject to the civil was still his creed, but it was
no longer the whole of it.   He began to see that for the
rule to hold good the civil power must be that which was
authorised by the Constitution; that it must be the power
to which the Government was entrusted by the country.
Since the deposition of the King and the abdication of
the Protector the constitutional civil power was the
Parliament, and the junto of politicians who were sitting
at Westminster was not the Parliament.   It was a truth
he would perhaps have been slower to grasp had they
treated him better in the matter of commissions; but they
had stupidly forced the situation home to the hard-witted
soldier, and having once embraced the idea he was not
likely to abandon it.   Nor was this all.   The man of the
hour was Lambert, his old rival, and the very apostle of
the doctrines he abhorred.   For Lambert the army was
a political body which had won the people their liberties,
and which alone was capable of administering them.   His
idea of the army was that it should be an executive
corporation as self-contained and independent as other
men at other times have sought to make the Church.
For this Cromwell had discarded him.   For this he had

come upon the scene once more, and the civil power
was in league with him.

Such was the light in which Monk viewed the situation when on August 8th his brother arrived at
Dalkeith. The general was as usual up to his eyes in
business. His ante-room was thronged with officers waiting for orders, and he had to commit Nicholas to the care
of Dr. Price. The two parsons soon fraternised. Nicholas
was bursting with his secret. The simple country rector
grew more and more nervous as the time went on. The
nearer the task of broaching the subject to his formidable
brother was approached the less he liked it. At last he
could contain himself no longer. Regardless of his oath
and Grenville's cautions, he blurted out his whole secret
and begged Price's assistance. The astute chaplain was
aghast at the negotiator's indiscretion, for not only had
he disclosed the western gentlemen's mission as Clarges
had authorised him, but he had let out Sir John Grenville's too. Fortunately Price was a Royalist, and no harm
was done. But he warned his simple visitor of the
atmosphere in which the general was existing. It was
a miasma of distrust and suspicion which none but
"honest George" could have breathed and lived. Every
eye was watching for a sign. The slightest indiscretion
might be fatal, and absolute secrecy was a necessity.
At the same time he gave him every encouragement.
Mrs. Monk, he said, was constantly urging her husband to
make a move, and he permitted her to talk the rankest
treason every night. In her he would certainly find an
active ally, and he himself would do his best. Finally
he told him the best way to approach the general. The
soldier was not without his superstitions, and Nicholas

was advised to pave the way for his disclosures with
some old wives' prophecies about the future greatness of
the family which he had brought out of Devonshire.

Thus prepared he was conducted to his brother. A
few officers were still waiting in the ante-room. One of
them at once suspiciously asked Price what was the
meaning of Nicholas's visit. Price put him off with the
story of Mary Monk, but nevertheless Nicholas was more
alarmed than ever, and began to see that conspiring was
not the simple affair of tokens and cyphers which he had
thought.

No one was present at the interview between the
brothers that evening, and no one knows exactly what
occurred, but it is certain that its effect was to give
George a much more serious view of the Great Design
than he had before. His contempt for Cavalier conspir-
acies was profound, and Grenville's message had probably
very little effect upon him. He did not know his young
cousin personally, and looked upon him merely as one more
of those enthusiastic young gentlemen whose sportive delight in hairbrained plots and whose passion for mystery
were always leading them into scrapes and indefinitely
postponing the Restoration. But Nicholas brought out
of Devonshire a message from a very different man.
Their kinsman, William Morice, had associated himself
with Stukeley and the other western gentlemen, and
Morice's administration of Monk's Devonshire estates
seems to have given the general a profound faith in that
gentleman's practical sagacity. Morice's approval at
least assured him that the Presbyterians were engaged,
and that Sir George Booth's rising was not a mere
Cavalier plot. He was already considerably impressed

by Lord Fairfax's adhesion, and now he began to see that whether or not the movement would end in the Restoration, the country was in earnest about having a real Parliament elected to settle some permanent form of government.

Nicholas gave Price such a favourable account of his interview that he looked upon the general as practically engaged. Still Monk gave no sign. Morice's advice involved, to say the least, putting pressure on the men whose commissions he held and whose pay he was taking. It was a serious obstacle, but everything continued to deepen the impression which Atkins and Nicholas had begun. Every post brought news that Booth's position was improving, and no doubt Mrs. Monk did her best when the curtains were drawn. Next week Colonel Atkins returned. Again he was well received, and Monk seems to have taken the opportunity of arranging a regular system of correspondence with Lord Fairfax, but nothing further appeared.

On Saturday the 23rd Dr. Gumble, chaplain to the Scotch commission, came over to Dalkeith, as he often did, to spend Sunday with the general and preach a sermon for Price. He was a staunch old Commonwealth man, who disapproved of the protectorate, but he was popular with the officers, highly esteemed by Monk, and so had kept his place. In him the perplexed general had a councillor who was above suspicion of Royalism. He took him into his confidence, put the whole case before him, and asked his advice. Gumble did not hesitate. He assured him that he had a higher duty than that which he owed to his paymasters. His country called to him to rescue her from the miserable

plight to which the clique of visionaries and self-seeking
politicians at Westminster had reduced her.   It was
his duty to obey the call.   To a man of Monk's ardent
patriotism such an argument could not appeal in vain.
It was the argument which finally convinced him it was
his duty to move.   Once resolved he characteristically
acted on the spot.   While he himself went to ascertain
the state of the Treasury, Gumble was despatched to
Price's room to inform him he was to draw up a manifesto ; and thence he proceeded to sound such officers as
were to be trusted.

The manifesto took the form of a respectful letter to
the Parliament, reminding them that they had not yet
filled up their numbers nor passed any Electoral Bill, as
the very name of Commonwealth required them, and
hinting that the army could not in conscience protect
their authority unless they forthwith remedied their
neglect.

On Sunday evening after service those already in the
secret assembled in Price's room to approve the manifesto.   It was resolved that it should be presented to the
army for signature, and the general proceeded to take
precautions against a refusal.   Captain Jonathan Smith,
his adjutant-general, had been admitted to the secret con-
clave.   Immediately the draft was settled Monk ordered
this officer to ride to the commandants of the neighbouring garrisons, who were all men of the right stamp,
explain to them the step that was to be taken, and
induce them to adopt the necessary measures for preventing the sectaries giving trouble.   The general then
left the room.   On the success of Smith's mission all
depended.   The army was full of doctrinaire politicians.

The Government in London had been careful to draft as
many as possible on to the Scotch establishment. These
men disliked and suspected Monk, and he had to rely
upon those who fought for their pay, by whom he was
generally beloved. Smith did not lose a moment. He
had already put on his boots, and was taking leave of
the rest when the door opened and the general came
into the room again. To every one's astonishment he
ordered Smith not to go. He had resolved, he said, to
wait the post in. By that time Lambert and Booth
must have met, and it could do no harm to hear the
result before they moved.

No one ventured to demur then, but Price presently
followed him from his room. He found him in earnest
conversation with his master of the greyhounds, one Kerr
of Gradane, one of Montrose's men, in whom Monk took
an interest that his love of coursing would hardly explain.
Price knew he had some other and more secret designs
to back his enterprise, and afterwards Monk told him he
had been ready to commission the whole Scottish nation
to rise. There can be little doubt that through Kerr he
was twisting another string for his bow as strong and
trustworthy as the first. "Old George" was not a man
to do things by halves.

Price waited till the conversation was done and Kerr
was out of hearing, and then he began to press the
general to allow Smith to start. Monk was anxious
and excited. For the first time in his life his military
conscience was not clear, and Price's importunity irri-
tated him past bearing. Turning on him fiercely he
seized him by the shoulders. "What, Mr. Price," said
he, "will you then bring my neck to the block for the

King, and ruin our whole design by engaging too rashly?"
—"Sir," protested the astonished chaplain, "I never
named the King to you either now or at any other
time."—"Well," replied the general, "I know you have
not. But I know you, and have understood your
meaning."

It was on this conversation, as Price relates it, that
Monk's biographers rely to prove their case that he
intended the return of the King from the first. But
there can be no doubt that what he said was to get rid
of Price by letting him clearly know he saw through
him, and had no intention of risking his head or spoiling
the patriotic enterprise in which he was engaged for
the sake of a Stuart.

At any rate it left Monk in peace. No move was
made that night, and early on Monday morning came
the startling news that Lambert had crushed Booth's
rising at a blow. Once more the confederates met,
burned the manifesto, renewed their oaths of secrecy,
and thanked Heaven for the narrow escape they had had.

Monk's feelings vented themselves in anger against
his brother and Grenville. He felt he had been deceived
and entrapped into a plot which had no more bottom
than the rest. He angrily told poor Nicholas to go back
to his books and meddle no more in conspiracy. He
charged him with a similar sharp message to his young
cousin, and swore if either of them ever revealed what
had passed he would do his best to ruin them both.
The affair seems to have been even a greater shock to
Mrs. Monk. Price hints that she conceived a sudden
antipathy for the King's cause, and lived in terror that
her husband would be induced sooner or later to engage

in it. She lost no opportunity of proclaiming that she
and her son Kit were for the Long Parliament and the
"good old cause," and she began again to urge Monk to
retire and live in Ireland. The general lent a willing
ear. The cashiering of his officers continued. Lambert
and the Rump seemed determined to pull together, and
every one thought the Government had a new lease of
life. Monk knew some attempt would soon be made
to displace him, and as he now had less inclination to
retain his post than ever he resolved to seize the opportunity of tendering his resignation on the ground of
ill-health and long service. He was certainly in earnest.
Thrifty Mrs. Monk bought a number of trunks to pack
up the household effects, and, contrary to his usual cus-
tom, the general wrote direct to the Speaker. Nicholas
fortunately warned Clarges that the letter had gone.
Clarges managed to get hold of it, took it himself to
Lenthal, and in concert with him cleverly arranged not
to have it presented to the House for some days; for
the commissary had news for his brother-in-law by which
he believed he could induce him to reconsider his determination.

CHAPTER X

IT is always a temptation to over-estimate the effect of trifling accidents in history, but certainly few little things have been fraught with weightier consequences than prudent "old George's" idea of waiting the post in. Had he made his great move while Rump and army were at one it is hard to say how long the Revolution might have dragged on its effete existence. It is indeed possible that he might still have succeeded in closing it, but it could only have been at the cost of a bloody civil war.

Now things were changed. Intoxicated with their success over the rebels, Lambert and Fleetwood, with the army-party, in a formal petition had made demands which it was impossible for the Rump to grant. Sir Arthur Haslerig, the hot-headed leader of the pure Republicans, had moved a vote of censure on Lambert, and Clarges was able to inform his brother-in-law that a breach was imminent. Monk at once instructed him to withdraw his resignation. He saw his duty clearly before him now, and waited quietly for news. The petition was forwarded to the Scotch army for signature, and its authors attempted to gain Monk over to their interest by

K

the offer of supreme command of the foot, and the rank of general in the standing army which they meant permanently to establish. His reply was to absolutely forbid a man under his command to sign the obnoxious document.

On September 27th another meeting of the English officers was held at which demands so extravagant were framed that the moderate men withdrew, and sent up to Monk imploring him to use his influence to prevent a breach. He did his best in a letter to Fleet-wood. But no one knew better than he that the attempt was useless, and his brother was hurried off to London with Mary Monk and a secret message to Clarges. No military scruples perplexed the old soldier now. His duty to his paymasters and his duty to his country were one. His commission stood no longer in the way of his patriotism or his political creed, and he spoke at last with no uncertain voice; for Commissary Clarges was charged to assure the House that if they would only stand firm in asserting their authority over the army he would stand by them, and be ready, should the need arise, to march into England to their defence.

With this message—the death-warrant of the English Revolution—Nicholas Monk reached London on October 11th. Over eleven years ago, in "the first year of freedom, by God's blessing restored," the chiefs of the army had met at Windsor to seek their duty from the Lord. In a long ecstasy of prayer and tears they had sought counsel of their God, and the answer came—the King must die. From that hour revolution had ridden triumphant on the shoulders of the army. But its day was done, its work was accomplished, and the most

perfect soldier of them all had risen up to enforce the
simple gospel of obedience. Prayer or no prayer, King
or no King, the soldier's duty was to obey, and not to
command.

For two days the House had been considering the
new petition from the army, determined not to grant
and afraid to reject it. The debate stood adjourned till
the morrow without hope of a solution to the problem.
It was late in the evening when Nicholas Monk reached
Clarges. In the first hours of the morning the commissary roused the Speaker and Haslerig with his news.
The whole situation was changed as if by magic. No
sooner was the House met than the tidings flew from
mouth to mouth, and in rapid succession a series of
votes were passed bidding defiance to Lambert and
the army. " Resolved that if they must leave their soft
seats they would first empty out the feathers," they
made it high treason to collect taxes without their
consent, cashiered Lambert, Desborough, and the seven
other colonels who were concerned in the movement,
deprived Fleetwood of the command of the army,
and vested it in a commission in which he was associated
with Monk, Haslerig, Ludlow, Morley, Walton, and
Overton, all staunch Parliament men. The following
morning Lambert had seized the approaches of the
House. Once more the Rump was the victim of a
coup d'état, and a military committee of safety reigned
in its stead.

Monk had foretold the quarrel months ago. On the
morning of the 17th the news for which he had been
waiting reached him at Dalkeith, and with startling
rapidity he set about backing his words. Never had

soldier a more difficult and dangerous task. In any one
of lesser calibre the attempt would be called madness.
He was face to face at last with his old rival. He was
about to defy the most brilliant of Cromwell's generals,
and before he could call his strength his own he had to
tear from it its toughest fibres. The London officers
had succeeded in making his army a hotbed of the very
opinions he had determined to crush with it. On the
whole Scotch establishment there was hardly a colonel
who was above suspicion. Every garrison and every
company were full of the veteran fanatics who had
taught the world the art of revolution, and every man of
them in his heart rejoiced at Lambert's success. With
this element free, his army was Lambert's army. At
all cost it must be made powerless, though it was the
very soul of his force. But Monk did not hesitate.
Not a moment was to be lost. In a few hours the news
would be all over Scotland and the chance gone.
All the principal garrisons, with the exception of
Stirling and Aberdeen, were in the hands of Lambert's
nominees, and the whole venture turned upon the
rapidity with which they could be secured.

Hardly was Clarges's despatch in the general's hands
when Captain Smith was galloping for Edinburgh and
Leith to take the first step towards mastering the garrisons there. The capital was occupied by Monk's own
regiment and Talbot's "Black Colours." Talbot's was
far from sound, and in the general's own there was
hardly an officer who was not a rank Anabaptist. Fortunately, in the absence of the superior officers, Talbot's
was being commanded by its major, Hubblethorne, and
Monk's by its senior captain, Ethelbert Morgan. At

Leith was "Wilkes's," also in charge of its major, Hughes; while in widely scattered quarters in the country round lay the general's own regiment of horse under Johnson, its senior captain.

These four men were summoned to Dalkeith and at once formed into a Council of War, together with such well-affected officers as Monk had managed to have about him in anticipation of the crisis. Their first step was to stop the post into England, and then far into the night they sat methodically but rapidly maturing every detail of the move. In the morning all was in working order. Two of the impromptu Council, who belonged to the garrisons at Perth and Ayr, were away at dawn to secure those fortresses. They were only captains, but in his hour of need Monk had hardly a single field-officer whom he could trust. At the same time Johnson was despatching orderlies right and left to concentrate the horse : Hubblethorne and Ethelbert Morgan were away again with secret orders; and far and wide messengers were spurring to summon the most dangerous officers to head-quarters, while small parties of horse were leisurely taking up their posts to waylay and arrest them as they came.

By dinner-time a troop of horse arrived at Dalkeith to escort the general to Edinburgh. He had determined to take the capital in hand himself, and as soon as he had dined he rode away. Meanwhile his secret orders had been carried out to the letter. He found his own regiment and Talbot's paraded in the High Street, and Captain Johnson in waiting with two more troops of his horse. Satisfied with his inspection the general rode on quietly to his quarters, and once there proceeded to

cashier nearly the whole of the officers of his own foot.
The command was given to Morgan, and Major Hubblethorne made lieutenant-colonel of the "Black Colours."
This done he returned to the High Street, and placing
himself at the head of the two regiments marched them
down to the open space before Greyfriars' Church. No
sooner were they again in line than he ordered the
arrest of the whole of the cashiered officers. Resistance
was out of the question. Monk's own had been paraded
without ammunition. The musketeers of the "Black
Colours" wore their bullet-bags and bandoliers ; the
sulphurous smell of their matches perfumed the air
with menace ; at the general's back were his faithful
troops of horse—and his order was obeyed.

Without giving his leaderless regiment a moment to
think Monk followed up the blow with a pithy and
soldier-like speech, asking them if they thought it right
for the Scotch army to submit to the insolent extra-
vagancies of the home forces. "For my own part," he
cried, "I think myself obliged by the duty of my place
to keep the military power in obedience to the civil.
Since we have received our pay and commissions from
the Parliament it is our duty to defend them. In this I
expect the ready obedience of you all. But if any do
declare their dissent to my resolution, they shall have
liberty to leave the service, and may take their passes to
be gone."

A thundering shout greeted his words. Not a man
was there but cried with wild enthusiasm he would
live and die for "old George." Edinburgh was won,
but the day's work was not yet over. As he left the
parade-ground a despatch was put into his hand. It

was from his friend Colonel Myers, the governor of
Berwick. The key of the London road was of the first
importance to Monk, and Myers declared he could not
hold it against the numerous Anabaptist officers in his
command. Monk immediately ordered a troop of horse
to his assistance; but a new difficulty arose. Berwick
was forty miles away. Not a trooper was in Edinburgh
who had not ridden twenty that day. The roads were
deep in mire, and every one declared the march impossible. It was a word Monk did not often listen to.
The march must be made. The general appealed to
Johnson as he only knew how, and as the night fell
the captain and his troop were spurring for the Border
through the Nether Bow Port.

Monk's drastic proceedings at Edinburgh were but a
type of what happened all over Scotland. By the time he
had in person secured and purged Leith and Linlithgow,
messengers began to pour into headquarters to report
that everywhere his promptitude had paralysed resistance.
Every garrison was in his hands and every high-road was
resounding with the tramp of the troops he had ordered
to concentrate on Edinburgh. There, too, Colonel Cobbett arrived a prisoner. It was Johnson's offering to his
general. It had been the first act of the Committee of
Safety to send up the colonel post-haste to secure not
only Berwick, but the Scotch army as well, and to arrest
Monk if he objected. A few hours before he reached
the Border Johnson's exhausted troop had toiled into
Berwick, and Cobbett arrived to find himself a prisoner.

Monk had now time to breathe. On the 20th the
post was allowed to go, and with it went three official
letters from the general. One was to the Speaker, lacon-

ically informing him that the Scotch army was at the
service of the Parliament if it were still under restraint, and that in accordance with his new commission
he had cashiered such officers as would not recognise its
authority.   "I do call God to witness," he concluded,
"that the asserting of a Commonwealth is the only
intent of my heart, and I desire if possible to avoid
the shedding of blood, and therefore entreat you that
there may be a good understanding between Parliament
and army.   But if they will not obey your commands I
will not desert you according to my duty and promise."

In the same strain he wrote to Fleetwood imploring
him to restore the Parliament.   "Otherwise," he says,
"I am resolved by the assistance of God, with this army
under my command, to declare for them and prosecute
this just cause to the last drop of my blood. . . . I do
plainly assure your lordship I was never better satisfied
with the justice of any engagement than in this. . . .
I desire your lordship not to be deluded by the specious
pretences of any ambitious person whatever."   He speaks
pathetically of his shame to see his country the scorn of
Europe, and again calls God to witness he has no other
end than the Restoration of parliamentary authority,
"and those good laws which our ancestors have pur-
chased with so much blood. . . . And I take myself so
far obliged, being in the Parliament's service, to stand
though alone in this quarrel."

The third letter was to Lambert.   He was "the ambitious person" on whom Monk had his eye; and
short and sharp as the letter was, he was careful to let
his old rival know that he suspected him of aiming at a
dictatorship.   He repeated his determination to stand

by the evicted Parliament; "for, sir," he concluded, "the
nature of England will not endure any arbitrary power,
neither will any true Englishman in the army, so that
such a design will be ruinous and destructive. Therefore I do earnestly entreat you that we may not be a
scorn to all the world and a prey to our enemies, that
the Parliament may be speedily restored to their freedom
which they enjoyed on the 11th of this instant."

These plain-spoken letters fell like thunderbolts
amongst the London officers. Fleetwood, Lambert, and
Desborough met at Whitehall in consternation. With
the short-sighted conceit of second-rate men they had
practically omitted Monk from their calculations. They
had mistaken his modest ambitions for indifference. The
Quixotic loyalty which had made him submit to the insolent orders of the war-office while Parliament was sitting,
they had taken for stupidity. Now with the suddenness of a dream this despised soldier of fortune, this
exalted drill-sergeant, as they thought him, towered like
a giant before them as the three politicians sat together
astounded. Midnight struck, and with the madness of
doomed men they sent for Clarges. The result of the
interview with Monk's subtle agent was that he and
Colonel Talbot were ordered to start for Scotland within
three hours to invite Monk to agree to an armistice
preliminary to settling their quarrel by a treaty.

Their action was none too prompt. They knew well
enough what to expect when Monk had once declared.
We know the importance he attached to the first rapid
moves of a campaign. Lambert at least was aware
of his methods, and knew he would not waste a moment.
Nor did he. No sooner were the Scotch garrisons safe

than a party of horse was sent to secure Carlisle, and
a small mixed column was pushed forward from Berwick
to surprise Newcastle. The attempt on Carlisle failed,
through the incompetency of the officer in command.
The Newcastle column came to a halt at Morpeth.
Colonel Lilburne, the man whom Monk had superseded
in Scotland, and who was now in command of the northern district, had thrown himself with a strong rein-
forcement into the threatened town. Determined to
avoid a conflict till he was ready, Monk ordered a retreat
to Alnwick.

As it happened, no accident could have been more fortunate for the success of Monk's designs. Had he taken
Newcastle, in a week it would have been besieged by
Lambert and Monk could not have moved to its relief.
Owing to the weather the Scotch army was concentrating
with exasperating slowness, and insubordination was by
no means at an end. Wholesale desertions began to take
place. Men were whispering that the general "had the
King in his belly." To stop their mouths he convened a
permanent Council of War and committed to it the whole
of his correspondence. He used the press freely, and
printed all his official letters. But difficulties seemed to
grow every day. The armies of England and Ireland
refused to join him, and the fleet followed their example.
In the midst of his perplexities Clarges arrived at Edinburgh, and showed him where his escape lay. The
Treasury in London was empty; Monk's was overflowing. Lambert must place his troops at free quarters,
and pay them with plunder. It was a mere matter of
time for the whole country to turn against him, and for
his army to melt away piecemeal. Immediate action was

Lambert's only game.   Every day he must grow weaker, while Monk was ever gathering new strength as troop after troop and company after company marched into Edinburgh from the Highlands.

In negotiation Monk saw the delay he needed.   His Council of War, being thoroughly averse to fighting their comrades who had bled for the old cause, embraced the idea with enthusiasm, and a commission, consisting of three colonels whom Monk trusted, was appointed to treat with the Committee of Safety.   A warm debate took place over the bases of negotiation.   The Council were inclined to ask for a new Parliament.   Monk insisted on the restoration of his masters, nor would he consent to the counter-proposition unless it were made contingent on the refusal of the Rump to sit.   Not content with this, he gave the commissioners secret instructions before they left not to disclose their power to treat for a new Parliament till the last moment.   For he well knew that Fleetwood and Lambert would never agree to restore the Rump if there was a possibility of a settlement on any other terms.   Having thus very cleverly thrown back the onus of a civil war on Lambert, while at the same time he had done his strict duty to his commission and his best to prolong the negotiations, Monk agreed to an armistice, and allowed the commission to depart.

At York they found Lambert with the head-quarters of the English army.   Professing an authority from the Committee of Safety, he made an effort to treat with them on the spot.   But mindful of their secret instructions they insisted on the question of the Parliament being first settled, and he was compelled to suffer them to proceed on their journey.

But even then his evil genius had not done with him. He felt that by allowing the negotiations to go forward he had removed one of his rival's difficulties. In a desperate effort to recover the ground he had thus lost he removed the other. All that Monk now required was a man whom he could trust to reorganise his army, and reduce it to the obedient machine of his ideal. The one man in the world to do it was his old comrade Morgan, who had recently returned from serving with the English contingent in the Low Countries under Turenne. He was still Major-general on the Scotch establishment, but had been laid up at York with gout. He was now recovered, and Monk had written to him to rejoin. The letter had been intercepted by Lilburne, and Morgan was still at York pretending to disapprove of the Scotch proceedings. His importance was well understood. Next to Monk he was considered the finest soldier in the three kingdoms. After his brilliant capture of Ypres, the great Turenne had embraced him on the shattered walls and told him with effusion he was amongst the bravest captains of his time. Yet this was the man that Lambert, with the fatuity of those whom Heaven has doomed, chose to send to Monk in order to induce him to lay down his arms.

What happened when the two old comrades met was only to be expected. Morgan delivered his message with a laugh, but never took back an answer. That was more than he had promised. He told his friend he had come to return to his duty, for he was no politician, and felt his best course was to follow a man whom he knew to be a true lover of his country.

The presence of the fiery little dragoon made itself

felt immediately. Cashiering and remodelling went on briskly, and so great was the enthusiasm which Morgan inspired that, in spite of the efforts of incendiaries from London, desertions entirely ceased. Without further anxiety Monk was able to devote himself to his statecraft. His correspondence at this time was enormous. Openly or in secret he was in communication with men of all shades of opinion, from constitutional Royalists like Lord Fairfax to pronounced Republicans like Haslerig. From all sides came envoys to expostulate or encourage. From Ireland Cornet Monk brought a message from the general's old comrades Coote and Jones, that they had every hope the Irish army would declare for him before long. The London Independents despatched delegates to mediate. Whatever the pretence, every one was trying to find out what the silent soldier intended. The burden of his answer was the same to all, that unless Lambert and his friends restored the Parliament, "he meant to lay them on their backs." For Haslerig and the Independents it was too much, for Lord Fairfax and the men of Booth's insurrection too little. The whole question was, what Parliament did he mean to restore? Was it the Long Parliament as it existed before Cromwell purged it of the Presbyterian Royalists, or was it the Republican Rump that was left when they were gone? The former meant a constitutional restoration; the latter a continuance of the republic.

But this alternative by no means sums up the political situation with which Monk suddenly found himself face to face. The complex condition of parties at this time is only comparable to that which exists in France to-day. In the place of the Legitimists were the old Cavaliers, in that of the Orleanists were the Moderate Royalists, who looked to a restoration by constitutional means. But there was this wide difference. Both monarchical parties supported the same dynasty, and together they formed the majority of the kingdom. They included practically the whole of the country gentlemen and all the Presbyterians of the Covenant. And whatever Monk might think of the expediency of a restoration, they represented the ideas which in his heart he regarded with the greatest favour. Next in strength and in Monk's sympathy was the party which corresponds to the French Moderate Republicans. It consisted of the old Commonwealth men, with Haslerig and Vane at their head, and was represented by the Rump, but it must be always remembered that they repudiated the idea of a president. For Napoleonists there were the Cromwellians, who, though now an exhausted and leaderless party, still clung to the principle of a protectorate. The field which the pure Opportunists occupy was filled by Lambert and his admirers, who, while they branded Haslerig as a reactionary, coquetted with the King. Together these two groups formed the right of the Army-party, which was held together by a vague policy of the supremacy of the military over the civil power. Its left looked to Fleetwood. Like the extreme left in France, this faction included men of a great variety of opinions, and in striking analogy to contemporary political phenomena, its moving spirits were the Anabaptists and Fifth Monarchy men, the Socialists and Anarchists of the time.

It is not of course pretended that the parallel is exact, but it is sufficiently close to bring the situation vividly before us; and when we remember that as in

France the parties were constantly combining into new groups, and further how complicated the whole position was by religious differences, it will serve as well as a detailed account to picture for us the labyrinth through which Monk was about to try and thread his way without violating the sacredness of his commission. No man ever approached a situation so difficult with so little experience or assistance. "Counsellor I have none to rely on," he is reported to have said at this time. "Many of my officers have been false, and that all the rest will prove true is too much gaiety to hope. But religion, law, liberty, and my own fame are at stake. I will go on and leave the event to God." No aim more patriotic was ever set up with more manly devotion. His success was then and still is regarded as an accident or a miracle. Be that as it may, in the whole roll of history there can be found no greater moral lesson than the story of the plain and steadfast purpose with which at last the end was won.

CHAPTER XI

By the middle of November the Scotch army was thoroughly remodelled and placed on its war-footing. Certain of the failure of the negotiations and regardless of the hardships of a winter campaign, on the 18th Monk began to move for the front. In his rear all was secure in spite of the denudation of the garrisons. Their fortifications had been freely dismantled, and by calling a Convention Parliament under the presidency of Glencairn he had come to a definite understanding with the Scots. So excellent were the relations he had established with them by his just and sympathetic government, severe as it was, that without holding out the slightest hope of a restoration he had received from them an undertaking that the country would not only remain quiet, but even assist him with a large force. The last offer he was prudent enough to refuse, fearing it would bring him under suspicion of Royalism.

The first halt was at Haddington. Everything had gone well, and the general was sitting down to supper with his officers amidst the hopeful excitement that marks the first move to the front. Hardly, however, had grace been said when some officers from London were announced. They presented the general with a packet. He tore it open where he sat, read it through, and then tossing it to his officers abruptly left the room without a word. With cries of rage they found it was a treaty into which their commissioners had been cheated and coerced, and which conceded to the Committee of Safety every point upon which the Scotch army had insisted.

It was a blow heavy enough to crush the stoutest heart, and at daybreak the general returned to Edinburgh, where the news had already raised a storm of fury. Officers crowded to head-quarters with despair and anger on their faces, and eagerly waited till Monk had done his breakfast. At last he strode into the ante-room and began walking up and down in sullen silence. Not a word was spoken till his confidant, Dr. Gumble, ventured to accost him. "What do you think of this agreement?" said the general abruptly. The doctor replied at once by asking leave to escape into Holland, for whatever the rest might hope he knew his life was not safe. "What!" cried Monk angrily, "do you lay the blame on me? If the army will stick to me I will stick to them." A burst of enthusiasm greeted his words. Every officer present vowed he would live and die with him, and shout after shout of joy re-echoed through the city as the news spread through the ranks of the soldiers.

A confidential council was called in the afternoon, and it was decided instead of repudiating the treaty to prolong the negotiations. To this end it was resolved to request a conference at Alnwick to explain doubtful points in the articles on the ground that they appeared to be inconsistent with the commissioners' instructions. Next morning a general advance to the Border was

L

ordered, and by the end of the month the head-quarters
were at Berwick. Another delay was gained, and to
prevent the possibility of a premature collision Monk
withdrew his outpost in Northumberland. Every day
some encouraging news added a fresh value to the
armistice. Clarges had returned to London, but before
he left Edinburgh Monk had told him that if he restored
the Parliament he should not feel it his duty to prevent
the secluded members resuming their seats. With this
the astute commissary had been able to satisfy Lord
Fairfax on his way south, and was now able to announce
that the Yorkshire gentlemen would be ready to rise for
a free Parliament by the middle of January. The old
Council of State had met in secret at the capital, and
sent down to Monk a commission as general of all the
forces in England and Scotland. Fleetwood was growing more suspicious of Lambert every hour, and in
his anxiety to come to an understanding with Monk
agreed to the proposed conference. Lambert was in
despair. His army at Newcastle was showing signs
of insubordination. Money was running short. The
ranks were full of sectaries devoted to Fleetwood. He
knew that further delay meant ruin, and he despatched
Colonel Zankey to Berwick with fresh proposals on his
own account to hasten the ratification of the treaty.
Zankey arrived early in December, in company with the
retreating outpost from Alnwick. In high spirits at
this new sign of discord in the enemy's camp the Council
met. A long bantering discussion ensued. Every argument which Zankey could urge was made light of, his
terms refused, and Monk, well satisfied with the day's
work, went to bed—but not to rest.

At one o'clock in the morning he was aroused with
alarming news.   A strong brigade of Lambert's cavalry
with two guns had seized Chillingham Castle, which was
but twenty miles from the Border.   Furious to think
that the precious armistice was broken, and still more that
Lambert should have taken advantage of the withdrawal
of the outposts to cover an advance with a flag of truce,
he ordered Zankey's instant arrest.   It was a fearful night.
The darkness was impenetrable and a storm was raging.
But at such a moment nothing mattered to the tough old
campaigner.   In an hour his orders for the army were
written, and he was galloping away recklessly to inspect
the fords uphill and downhill along the frozen roads, regardless of the protests of his staff.   "It was God's
infinite mercy we had not our necks broke," wrote one
of them afterwards.   At Norham the storm had increased
to such a fury that he was compelled to take shelter in
the castle.   By daylight, however, he had visited every
pass over the Tweed, and a little before noon he reached
Coldstream, where he intended to make his head-quarters.
Here was the best ford over the river, and he had ordered
a strong force to muster for its protection.   So well had
his orders been obeyed that he found his troops had already consumed everything that was fit for food or drink
in the place.   But "old George" was as indifferent to
hunger as he was to fatigue.   In dismay his staff saw him
sit down in a small cottage and quietly take out a quid
of tobacco.   It was for him all that Captain Bobadil
boasted.   His staff stole away to hunt for a dinner, and
when they returned the general was still serenely chewing where they had left him.

Lambert's supposed advance had proved a false alarm.

It was but an unauthorised raid for plunder. But it was enough to show the old strategist his danger. If Lambert had the sense or power to make a dash over the Border with his thousands of horse and mounted infantry, Monk was so weak in those arms that he would be compelled to retreat, and retreat meant ruin. Everything depended on a strong defensive position, and with consummate skill he marked one out. The bulk of the little army was stationed on the right at Kelso, and intrusted to Morgan, who had orders to exercise it daily in the general's pet formation of mixed files of horse and foot. From Kelso as far as Berwick every pass was occupied, and the troops quartered in the neighbouring villages and farmsteads. Yet within four hours, so nicely was every detail adjusted, the whole force could be concentrated on a given point. The position was practically impregnable. The desolate character of the country in its front rendered an attack in force impossible. Even if Lambert could have induced his pampered army to move, he could not have fed them for the time a concentration would take in the fearful weather that prevailed. If he attempted a turning movement by the Carlisle road Monk would get three days' start in London, and the Scotch army was too strong to be checked by any force that Lambert could safely detach from his main body.

To perfect his masterly disposition Monk established himself in the centre at Coldstream. His quarters were a smoky little thatched cottage with but one room. His bed was so small that he used it as a pillow, with his legs and body resting uneasily on benches. Indeed he and his officers suffered here every hardship that bad lodging, worse food, and intense cold could inflict; but such was the spirit which the general's example infused that the only effect of their sufferings was to arouse a cheery spirit of freemasonry among them. Till their dying day it was their pride to be called Coldstreamers. They never ceased to bore their friends with Coldstream stories, nor tired of joking about the chapel in the cowhouse and the beer that went bad before it got cold.

Severe as were their privations, for the rest of the year they had to bear them with as much of the general's equanimity as they could attain. As for him, he never left his quarters for a night except once, to meet the delegates of the Scots Convention at Berwick for the final settlement of the affairs of the interior while he was away. For the rest comfort was not wanting. The colder it grew the more difficult it was for Lambert to move, and if good liquor was scarce, good news flowed in plenty through the secret channels which Clarges had laid. In London riots were being suppressed with bloodshed, and mutiny was threatening at Newcastle. The Fanatics of Fleetwood's party, of whom the army was full, began to distrust Lambert's ambition, while Monk's judicious refusal to allow the Scots to arm restored the confidence of those who had hitherto suspected him of malignancy. The Irish regiments had not forgotten him; the Parliament's guards were plainly inclined to its champion; at head-quarters mutinies daily alarmed the Council; and Fleetwood's only idea of restoring discipline was to fall on his knees at the head of the disaffected regiments and say his prayers.

Still the negotiations could not be prolonged for ever, ingenious as was the committee which Monk had appointed to carry them on. It was therefore an immense relief when tidings came that the governor of Portsmouth had opened his gates to Haslerig, Morley, and Walton. Monk at once sent to Lambert to say that as three of his fellow-commissioners had returned to their duty he could not continue the negotiation without consulting them. "He has not used me well," said poor Lambert, and refused to grant a pass to Portsmouth. Monk's messenger had to return, but not empty. He came bursting with news. Vice-Admiral Lawson had declared for Monk's programme, and the fleet was threatening to blockade the Thames. In the same hour from Portpatrick arrived an officer to tell how the general's old comrades had seized Dublin Castle, and that the Irish army was ready to assist him actively. In the midst of the thanksgivings for these mercies a kinsman of Lord Fairfax stole over the hills to announce that the Yorkshire gentlemen would be ready to fall on Lambert's rear by New Year's Day, and at the Yorkshire general's request Monk promised to watch Lambert "as a cat did a mouse," and to advance to their assistance the moment there was a sign of a movement against them.

Indeed things were going almost too well. Price grew alarmed that the Rump was going to triumph completely, and though his dangerous presence was tabooed by Monk he stole into head-quarters in the dead of night. Rousing the weary soldier from his uneasy couch he implored him to remember the "old known laws." "Mr. Price," said Monk passionately, "I know your meaning, and I have known it. By the grace of God I will do it if ever I can find it in my power; and I do not much doubt but that I shall." Then seizing both his chaplain's hands he said again, " By God's help

I will do it." It is perfectly clear that Monk's love for his country inspired him with a desire to see monarchy re-established by a free Parliament as the only durable settlement, and that at this moment he was very hopeful about it.[1] It is equally certain he did not intend to restore Charles by force; and even if a Stuart were in his eyes worth a drop of English blood, even if he had had any faith in a settlement that was founded in civil war, his creed was still unshaken, and he meant so far as in him lay to keep the army from meddling with the civil power. He held the commission of the Rump, and had signified his intention to be loyal to it by signing a manifesto of the army by which he bound himself to restore the Parliament as it was before the late *coup d'état*.

Price's anxiety was but too well justified. On the last day of the year a messenger came ploughing through the snow to Coldstream with startling news. Fleet-wood's army had mutinied. "The Lord had spit in his face." He had given up the game, and the Rump was sitting again at Westminster. Fortunately it was not the end of the tidings. Fairfax had been compelled to rise prematurely, owing to the discovery of his plot, and Monk promptly issued orders for the little army to concentrate on Coldstream. Despatch after despatch interrupted his preparations. Lilburne's regiment had deserted to Fairfax, and the whole Irish Brigade had followed its example. It was clear that Lambert's only chance was a swift back-stroke at Fairfax, and Monk determined to anticipate the intelligence he hourly ex-pected. As the first gray beams of the year 1660

[1] Cf. Sir Phil. Warwick's opinion quoted by Kennett, *Hist.* iii. p. 217.

began to streak the leaden sky they lit up a memorable picture. Erect in his saddle amidst the trampled snow sat the warlike figure of the great soldier of fortune, on whose sagacity hung the destiny of Britain; and past him filed rank after rank the vanguard of his toil-stained troops as they strode cheerily on to cross the white plain of the frozen Tweed.

The famous movement had begun. Colonel Knight, by a splendid march through the snow, reached Morpeth with the vanguard the same evening. Finding Lambert had fallen back against Fairfax, he continued his advance, and the following morning surprised and seized Newcastle at break of day. The general followed with the rest of the army. All told it consisted of but four weak regiments of horse and six fine ones of foot. It was divided into two brigades, one under himself and the other under Morgan. The first night they reached Wooler, and heard officially from the Speaker of the restoration of the Rump, and unofficially that Lambert, deserted by his army, had disappeared. The Speaker's letter contained an acknowledgment of Monk's services, but no orders. He therefore ignored his unofficial intelligence and continued his advance. On the 4th he reached Morpeth, where he was received by the Sheriff of Northumberland. Next day arrived from London the City Sword-bearer with a petition from the Lord Mayor and Corporation that he would declare for a full Parliament, as they were unrepresented in the Rump. A deputation from the Newcastle municipality invited him to the town, and accordingly he entered it amidst the first of those ovations which were to mark every step of his memorable march.

Yet in spite of the enthusiasm that his soldierly figure excited whenever it appeared in the streets, Monk could not congratulate himself on his position. He had practically failed. Instead of giving his country a free Parliament he had restored the Rump. For England he saw nothing but new political troubles, for himself a repetition of the suspicion and ingratitude he had already experienced. Still he held their commission, and felt bound to do his duty to them. All else was dark before him. So Dr. Gumble was sent to London to convey his compliments and humble advice to the authorities, and as secretly as possible to see what could be made out of the situation. Nor did he depart further from the path of duty than to allow an officer to proceed to his old comrades in Ireland, suggesting that the Irish army should petition for a free Parliament.

From Coldstream, as soon as he heard the Rump was sitting, he had written to the Speaker for orders. As yet none had arrived, and he determined, in pursuance of his new authority as commander-in-chief, to advance to York. There he arrived on the 11th, to find no trace of Fairfax or his party. They had disappeared, and the city was in the hands of troops who had gone over to the Parliament. The rest of Lambert's deserters had joined the Yorkshire gentlemen, but had sent to the right-about every Cavalier that had shown himself at the rendezvous. Buckingham himself, Fairfax's own son-in-law, had had to go in spite of his irreproachable professions. York had refused to receive any of Fairfax's partisans. Lord Fairfax himself, sensible of a fiasco, had made a fit of the gout an excuse for retiring to his own house. However, on Monk's arrival he en-

tered the city in state to see him. With every argument he urged him to stay where he was and declare
for the King. Monk of course refused, but he could not
prevent his association with Fairfax arousing the old
suspicions. No means was omitted to clear himself.
An officer was heard to say that Monk would at last
bring in Charles Stuart, and the old general, in a fit
of exasperation, publicly gave him a sound thrashing
for his pains.

Still these suspicions were not without their value.
The Rump shared them. They dare not leave him with
Fairfax; they dare not order him to retreat. There was
no course but to tell him to advance, and Monk obeyed
with alacrity. Sending Morgan back to keep Scotland
quiet, and leaving Colonel Fairfax to occupy York,
he marched on the 16th with an army increased, by
a careful selection from Lambert's deserters, to nearly
six thousand men. His progress was a triumph. The
peasantry thronged to the highway to stare at the
deliverer as he passed. The church-bells rang. The
gentry came in troops with addresses, urging on him
the necessity of a full Parliament. Silent as a sphinx,
the harassed soldier rode on through it all, while all the
world watched him. Every eye, every ear, was strained
for a sign; and a safe platitude or two about his country's
welfare and the duty of his place was all that could be
dragged from his impenetrable reserve.

As he advanced his perplexities and his silence increased. On the 18th Gumble met him at Mansfield to
say that already half the House were his declared enemies.
An oath for the abjuration of the Stuart dynasty had
been imposed upon the new Council of State, of which

he had been made a member. An attempt, however, to
order its administration to the House had led to a determined resistance from the best of the old Commonwealth
men. The House was split into two factions, and Monk's
popularity with the non-abjurers was but adding to the
suspicions of the abjurers. At Nottingham Clarges
arrived to confirm and add to Gumble's intelligence. A
deputation, consisting of Scot, the new Secretary of State,
and Robinson, another abjuring member of the Government, was on its way to offer him the congratulations
of the House, but with secret instructions to watch his
every movement and endeavour to entrap him into abjuring. The London garrison, too, had by no means acquiesced
in Fleetwood's surrender, and was still in a state of sullen
hostility. It was clear that the crisis was not yet at an
end, and there was still hope for Monk, that if he could
once establish himself in London and keep things quiet,
one party or the other would force on a general election.
The chief difficulty was Fleetwood's army. It was
stronger than Monk's, and out of its entire roll only two
foot regiments, Morley's and Fagg's, could be trusted.
Ashley Cooper had a regiment of horse, but it certainly
would not obey him. Fortunately in the House the
non-abjurers were in the majority, and at Clarges's suggestion Monk used his few remaining hours of liberty to
prepare a letter to the Speaker pointing out the advisability of removing from about the Parliament the regiments which were as yet hardly cool from rebellion.

On Monday the 22nd he continued his march, and
before Leicester was reached Scot and Robinson appeared.
From that moment he could not call his soul his own.
By day they had him to ride in their coach, by night

they bored holes in the partitions that separated their room from his. They got up discussions at meals and stood at his elbow while he received the endless deputations and addresses that were showered in his path. All was of no avail. The old soldier stuck to the plain rule that had served him so well through life, and was not to be caught. Finding the situation was getting beyond him, he patiently resumed his unassailable position of the obedient and disinterested soldier of fortune. He received the commissioners as his superior officers. The troops had orders to halt and present arms whenever their coach passed, and in every way they were treated with the ceremony reserved for a commander-in-chief. The commissioners were delighted, and sent glowing accounts to the Speaker. They even accepted the general's excuse for not at once taking the Oath of Abjuration. He had understood, he said, that some members of the Government had refused it, and he felt it was better to wait till he got to London and could hear both sides.

The deputations from the city and the counties that met him at every town as he proceeded knew not what to make of it. The general received them with the utmost civility, and the commissioners railed at their petitions. The principal points they variously urged were a full and free Parliament, a dissolution, and the admission of the members secluded in 1648 without any previous oath or engagement. Sometimes the general found himself compelled to answer them. If the Parliament were not yet free, he told them, he would endeavour to remove the restraint that remained. The House had already decided to fill up the vacant places, and then it would be full. It had agreed to dissolve itself of its

own accord, and as for admitting members to sit without
any engagement to the Government, such a thing was
never heard of, and besides, the House had decided not
to readmit them.   And he politely expressed his surprise
that they thought him capable of so far forgetting his
duty to his commission as to question the resolution.
Thoroughly disheartened the deputations retired to fall
into the hands of enthusiastic staff-officers, who filled
them with new wonder.   Monk seems to have told his
friends to do their best to remove any bad impression his
reception of the addresses might arouse, and they interpreted their instructions with some freedom.   Lavish
promises were made in the general's name, and every one
was told to proceed actively with the petitioning without
paying the slightest attention to what Monk pretended to
think of them.

So the people only shouted more loudly and the bells
rang more merrily as the triumph went on through
Harborough, Northampton, Dunstable, till on the 28th
St. Albans was reached.   Here a halt was made to allow
the columns to close up and for the crucial request to be
made.   For Monk determined from here to despatch the
letter which had been prepared at Nottingham.   Clarges
was sent on before to pave the way for its reception.   It
was a critical moment.   The House had just confirmed
Monk's commission of general.   It was a rank then considered so dangerously exalted as to be hardly ever conferred.   Indeed before the Revolution it had seldom been
borne except by the sovereign, and already the *quidnuncs*
began to talk of his alliance with the Plantagenets.   It
was the very point upon which the leaders of the army
had finally broken with Parliament, and the first act of

Monk in his new capacity was to request that the whole
of Fleetwood's troops might be removed from the capital
to make way for his own.

A violent debate ensued. Haslerig opposed it with all
his weight, but so well organised were the non-abjurers
and so favourable had been Scot's reports that the
request was granted. The great difficulty was overcome, and on February 2nd Monk moved to Barnet.
That night for the first time the commissioners slept in
another house. Apparently they intended to make one
despairing effort on the part of the abjurers to keep
Monk from peacefully occupying the capital. At all
events about midnight the Secretary of State rushed into
Monk's quarters in his night-shirt and slippers crying
that the apprentices were out and the garrison in mutiny.
He implored, he commanded Monk to march on the spot
and restore order, but the old general was perfectly
unmoved. He grimly told him he would undertake to
be in London early enough in the morning to prevent
mischief, and Scot had to go back to bed. Some considerable disturbance there had been, but before Monk
marched next day it had been easily suppressed by a
few troops of horse and something on account of arrears.

Next night there was high feasting at Westminster.
Weeks ago at Holyrood Monk's butler had promised the
staff a bottle of wine at Whitehall on Candlemas Day.
He was a wag whom Charles the First had mock-knighted
one evening at supper with his table-knife in the old days
at Oxford. It was only a day late, and "Sir" Ralph Mort
was called on to pay his wager as the general sat with
the Coldstreamers in the "Prince's Apartment" rejoicing
at the success of their move. Everything had gone well.

Days before at Nottingham the details of the occupation had been arranged, and the troops had quietly marched to their quarters without a hitch. True the Coldstreamers' reception had not been enthusiastic. In vain had Monk ridden down Chancery Lane and the Strand at the head of his army, with trumpeters and led horses and all the pomp of a general in the field. In vain was his staff swelled by a brilliant crowd of gaily-dressed gentlemen. For the thoughtful the general's intentions were too dark : for the thoughtless his troops were too shabby ; and the entry was made with the cold precision of an operation of war.

CHAPTER XII

ON THE WINGS OF THE STORM

WITH Monk's success his real difficulties began. His first act was to attend the Council of State. The Oath of Abjuration was tendered to him and he refused it. A third of the Council had done the same, and amongst them irreproachable Republicans. He suggested a conference between the two parties to settle the point. For the present he certainly could not take it. He must consult the Coldstreamers. "The officers of my army," he said, and his words must have sounded strangely like a threat, "are very tender in taking oaths." So he returned to his apartments to be besieged with callers. Politicians were there eager for a word on which to work, and astute foreign ministers at their wits' end what to report to their respective governments. For every one a discreet answer had to be provided. All Sunday the game continued with little relief, except a secret information that Scot's son had been boasting how in a few days the general would be in the Tower with his head in danger.

Monk wisely took no more notice of the information than to display his force by lining the way from White-hall to Westminster with a "triumphant guard" as on

Monday he went down in state to receive the thanks of
Parliament. Scot had told him that a declaration of
his devotion to the House and his dislike of the addresses
was expected. It was a trying ordeal, but his blunt
honesty took him through. A chair of state had been placed
for him at the bar, but he refused to sit, as unbecoming
a servant of the Parliament. Standing he received the
fulsome vote of thanks, and then leaning over the back
of the chair, he made his modest acknowledgments, pro-
testing he had done no more than his duty. As though
he were making an official report of matters in which he
had no personal concern, he told them that on his way to
town he had observed the country to be very anxious for
a settlement, and that a number of addresses had been
presented to him. The demands they contained and his
own unexceptionable answers were summarised with
soldier-like brevity. "But although I said it not to
them," he continued, "I must say (with pardon) to you;
that the less oaths and engagements are imposed (with
respect had to the security of the common cause) the
sooner your settlement will be attained to. . . . I know
all the sober gentry will close with you if they may be
tenderly and gently used. And I am sure you will so
use them; as knowing it to be the common concern to
amplify and not lessen our interest, and to be careful that
neither the Cavalier nor the Fanatic party have a share
in your civil or military power." In conclusion he
respectfully called attention to the advisability of con-
firming the land-grants of the Irish soldiers and adventurers, and of settling several points for the better and
more equable administration of Scotland.

Nothing could have been done better. The imme-

diate effect of the speech was an immense increase in
Monk's popularity.   The conservative Republicans were
delighted at his deferential demeanour; their ladies, returning from Mrs. Monk's reception at Whitehall, approved her sweetmeats, and complacently noted how
she had helped them to wine with her own hand; while
the country at large read the general's speech as a threat
to the oligarchy which oppressed it.   The city was enthusiastic, for not only did it begin to doubt the sin-
cerity of his devotion to the Rump, but by his conclusion
about Ireland the capitalists saw in him their champion.
And, as we have seen, at such a crisis the capitalists had
then the same peculiar influences which they have exercised under similar conditions in more modern times.

In fact from this moment the city became the scene
on which the drama of the Restoration was to be played
out.   A week ago Mordaunt had arrived on a special
mission from Charles to assure the Corporation of his
constitutional intentions should he return, and the city
had definitely turned its face to the King.   The situation which the prevailing political uncertainty had
brought about was no longer endurable.   Trade was in
a state of complete stagnation.   Property was felt to
be unsafe.   The city was without a single representative
in Parliament.   It saw the moment had come for a
decisive step, and two days after Monk's speech, on the
ground that the sitting Parliament was not a representative assembly, the Common Council resolved to
pay no more taxes till the House had filled up its
vacancies.

Monk's principles were immediately put to a severe
test.   It was late at night when the vote of defiance

became known at Whitehall, but a summons came for
his instant attendance at the Council of State. The
hours went by and he did not return. His friends
remembered young Scot's boast, and gathered in alarm.
Ashley Cooper tried to take his seat in the Council-
chamber, but found it locked and guarded. Mrs. Monk
hammered on the door and cried frantically to her
husband, but not a sound came back. In despair she
retired to her apartments, and it was past two before
she was relieved by her husband's reappearance. Then
it was only for a moment. To his friends' dismay he
briefly told them that at daybreak the city was to be
occupied, and then refusing to listen to any one went
to bed. His paymasters had ordered him to coerce
those on whom all his hopes depended, and he was
going to obey.

The movement was punctually carried out, and no
sooner were the guards set and the troops at their
quarters than Monk, in accordance with his instructions, sent for a number of the leading citizens and
placed them under arrest. This done, to the amaze-
ment of his officers, he ordered them to remove the city
gates and portcullises, and the post and chains by which
the streets were barricaded. In vain they protested, in
vain his most devoted followers tendered their commissions. His only reply was to order the subordinate
officers to do the work of their superiors. Of so astound-
ing a piece of obedience no one knew what to think.
The common soldiers were inclined to look upon it as
a joke; the officers were in despair. At last a deputation of the Corporation waited on him to expostulate,
and promise that if he would desist the Common Council

would meet early on the morrow and reconsider its determination.

Monk at once complied, and reported to the Council of State recommending a lenient course. They replied brutally that they had dissolved the Common Council, and that he was not only to take down the gates but to break them in pieces. Again he obeyed. "Now, George," cried Haslerig when he heard of it, "we have thee for ever, body and soul." On the morrow, with growing anger, the troops recommenced the hateful work. They fraternised with the people, and together they railed at the Rump. Morley, who held the Tower, came and offered to declare against the men of Westminster if Monk would only give the word. His warmest friends went to reason with him, but the general sat in his quarters at the Three Tuns, near Guildhall, grimly chewing his tobacco, and no one dare speak to him. So extraordinary was his conduct that his officers began to believe he had some deep design. The orders were carried out to the last letter; guards were set at all the important points, and in the afternoon the rest of the army marched back to its quarters about Westminster.

Haslerig and his friends had won an incalculable victory. On Monk hung the hopes of the country, and they had deliberately struck him a fatal blow where they knew his spotless sense of honour exposed him without defence to their attack. His position was indeed desperate, and no sooner was he alone at White-hall than Clarges came in to point out the extremity of his danger. The wanton insult he had put upon the liberties of the great municipal corporation must turn

against him not only every town in the kingdom, but
the whole influence of finance and commerce. It was
the deliberate intention of the Council that it should.
Nothing could now save him but to return immediately
to the city and declare for a free Parliament. Monk
would not listen. Clarges in desperation began to urge
the folly of being true to men who did not keep their
side of the engagement. He showed the general how
through the whole affair he had been treated with contempt. Ever since his entry into London the Government had habitually called him "Commissioner" Monk.
They had denied him the very rank they themselves
had conferred upon him, and violated the commission on
which he based his obedience. The general began to
waver. He felt the injustice keenly, and confessed at
last that something must be done to regain the country's
esteem. With that he dismissed his kinsman, saying
that he would take till Tuesday to consider what course
he should adopt.

It was Friday. By Tuesday the news would be all
over the kingdom and he a ruined man. It was absolutely necessary to do something at once. Presently
Clarges returned with Dr. Barrow, the general's private
physician and judge-advocate, a man who had been of
great service throughout. Two or three officers accom-
panied them, with whom they had privately agreed to
brave the general's displeasure in one more effort to
save him from his rigid integrity. With the vehemence
of despair they poured out proof after proof of the
Rump's iniquitous intentions. Haslerig was in correspondence with Lambert. Ludlow, whom Monk had
accused of treason on Coote's information, still sat in

his place.   A tumultuous petition in favour of strict
abjuration had been fomented and received by the
House at the hands of Praise-God Barebones himself,
the ringleader of those very fanatics against whom he
had come to act.   The Council was even then, it was
said, considering whether they should cashier him on
the ground that in leaving the city he had disobeyed
its orders.   After all his devotion it was more than the
honest soldier could endure, and reluctantly he consented to march into the city next day.   Having issued
his orders accordingly, he told his little council to prepare some excuse to the Parliament.   No excuse could
be found.   The general was worn out; for the last
two nights he had had no sleep; unable to resist any
longer, he at last allowed a letter to be prepared, setting
out the real reasons of the movement and demanding
the House to keep its word.   With that he went to
bed, and all through the night the four councillors that
remained were busy with the manifesto.

Early next morning the members came down to the
House in the ordinary course.   The guards were all on
duty as usual, and the Speaker proceeded to take the
chair.   No sooner, however, was business begun than two
of Monk's colonels came in with a long letter signed by
the general and fourteen of his field-officers.   In respectful but unequivocal language it charged them with deliberately seeking to undo all the good that had been effected
by their restoration.   It desired them, therefore, to show
their good intentions by settling the qualification of
members and issuing writs for the vacant seats by the
next Friday.   It reminded them that the date fixed for
their dissolution was at hand, and finally informed them

that with the intention of waiting for their "full and free concurrence to these just desires of the nation," and of preserving order till it was obtained, the army had retired into the city.

The House was thrown immediately into a tumult of consternation. At the very moment when their terrible slave seemed safely bound he had risen up and snapped his chains like threads. Every kind of proposition was made to recall him, but eventually Scot and Robinson were ordered to carry a soft answer into the city. They found Monk with the Lord Mayor, and in the lowest spirits. His reception had been more than cold; the city had lost faith in him; he had broken the guiding rule of his life and had lost faith in himself. His friends urged him to declare at once for a free Parliament, but hoping against hope that he still might not be forced to use the military power against the civil, he refused to give a hint of his intended revolt till he heard the answer of the House. When it came, shifty and meaningless, he doubted no longer. Without heat he dismissed the messengers, but his officers insulted them, and the mob hooted them out of the city. Once more himself, blunt and determined, he stood up in the Guildhall to address the Council which the Lord Mayor had consented to call at five o'clock. With manly frankness he told them how he detested the work he had had to do. If laying down his commission would have stopped it, he would gladly have done so, but it would only have been put into unkinder hands. "But what I have to tell you," he concluded, "is that this morning I have sent to the Parliament to issue out writs within seven days for the filling up of their House, and when filled to sit no longer

than till May 6th, that they may give place to a full
and free Parliament."

The enthusiasm with which his words were received
was indescribable. As the news spread through the city
the people gave way to the wildest demonstrations of
joy. Late as it was the bells were set a-ringing; the
soldiers, who had been shivering all day in their ranks
on Finsbury Fields, were brought in to be fed and fêted
like kings. Bonfires were soon blazing in every street,
and anything that could do duty for an effigy of the
Rump was cast into them. To such a pitiable decrepi-
tude had the glorious Long Parliament lived.

As its doom was cried from end to end of England
the same extravagant scenes were enacted. Associations
were everywhere formed to refuse the payment of taxes
till Monk's demands were complied with. Everywhere
men were worshipping the executioner of their doting
liberator. His guards kept watch at the Parliament's
gates; from the city his sword was stretched over it.
In spite of himself, in spite of every effort to set a lawful
authority above him, George Monk was uncrowned King
of England.

But the sternest of those who had made the renown
of the greatest of Parliaments were still in their places,
and it was soon clear that they meant to leave no stone
unturned to dethrone their enemy. Persuasion having
failed they tried what force could do. A new commission for the army was appointed, so arranged that Monk
must always be in the minority. They distributed arms
to the Fanatics; they tampered with his troops; they industriously spread reports amongst Fleetwood's army that
Monk and the city were in league to restore the King.

Monk's complete reply was to seize the arms of Cavaliers and Fanatics alike and to refuse to allow the city to mobilise its militia. Then they fell to coaxing again, with no more success. For Monk began to see a better way of ridding himself of the power which had fallen on him than by surrendering it on any terms to those who had so misused it.

Ever since he had established himself at Draper's Hall addresses and petitions of all kinds had flowed in upon him. It soon appeared that the great majority of them were in favour of escaping from the deadlock by the restoration of the secluded members. To this the general had always been averse. They were pronounced Royalists, who wished to go back to the Isle of Wight treaty and the *status quo* of 1648, regardless of the vested interests that had arisen meanwhile. It meant the resumption of the land-grants which had been made for the services of those who had shed their blood for the good old cause, and that in Monk's eyes meant a new civil war. Already the suspicions which his understanding with the city had aroused were once more driving the Republicans into the extended arms of Lambert's militarism, and he seems to have at this time regarded the objections to the King's return as insuperable. Milton with all his eloquence, and Haslerig with all the ardour of his democratic faith, were blinding him to everything but the "good old cause." "From my soul I desire a Commonwealth," he wrote to Haslerig, and so long as the secluded members showed themselves irreconcilable to the Republic he would have nothing to do with them. Now, however, it was suggested to him that they were willing to come to terms with the sitting members, and he permitted a conference between the victims and the instigators of Pride's Purge.

The conference was so far satisfactory that the general entered into direct negotiations with the secluded members on behalf of the army. The chief points on which he insisted were a clear understanding that nothing was to be done to change the form of government from a Commonwealth; that the House should dissolve immediately it had provided for the interim administration of the country; and that the land-grants should be confirmed. On the first two points their answer was satisfactory. The last they rejected on the ground that they had no authority to pass such an act. Were any proof wanted of the disinterestedness of Monk's conduct at this time, it is that in spite of his undeniable love of money he gave up the point on which hung the hard-earned savings of a lifetime. Yet even this risk he was prepared to run for the good of the country he loved so well. Early on February 21st all the secluded members who were in town assembled at Whitehall. There the general met them and made them a speech setting forth his view of the situation. He told them that monarchy was not to be thought of. The old foundations were so broken that they could not be restored. If the nation found their long struggle was only to end in a restoration they would never again be induced to rise for the liberties of Parliament, and the cause of freedom would be lost for ever. Besides a King meant bishops, and that the country would never endure again. So he dismissed them to Westminster under the escort of his own lifeguard.

Almost the first act of the reinvigorated Parliament

was to name Monk "Captain-General under Parliament of all the land forces in England, Scotland, and Ireland." By virtue of this exalted rank he became as fully as the sovereign of to-day the constitutional head of the nation in arms. Added to this he was made jointly with Montague general of the fleet, and when the list of the new Council of State came out his name appeared in large type across the top like a king's. Haslerig at once saw his opportunity for a new departure. To destroy Monk's power directly was no longer possible, but so exalted was his position that could it be forced a little higher it would become insecure; or if the worst came to the worst, a protectorate, or even a King George, was better than the accursed Stuart.

This dangerous move on the part of the Common-wealth men soon began to show itself. A pamphlet had already appeared setting out Monk's royal descent. Now an insidious motion was made in the House to bestow on him and his heirs for ever the palace of Hampton Court and all its parks, and a Bill to give it effect was success-fully brought in. But before long a still better oppor-tunity presented itself to Haslerig. On March 13th the House, on the plea of leaving the nation absolutely free, abrogated the "Engagement" which members had to take to be true and faithful to the Commonwealth as established without King or House of Lords. Monk was highly annoyed. He looked upon it as a breach of the conditions on which the secluded members had been admitted. Jealous of his principles, he had seated them with a high hand on the express understanding that nothing was to be done to alter the constitution. Prac-tically the vote went far to make him and the army responsible for the counter-revolution to which it directly pointed, and which every day looked more unavoidable. Haslerig saw the moment had come to play his trump card. With the concurrence of their party and a number of officers, he, Scot, and some others repaired to White-hall, bent on inducing Monk to assume the protectorate. Clarges was first sounded. He gave no encouragement, and the conspirators left him to go straight to the lord-general. In alarm lest his brother-in-law's power of resistance should be unequal to so splendid a temptation, Clarges flew to the Council which was sitting in a room close by. In answer to an urgent summons Ashley Cooper came out, and Clarges hurriedly told him his alarming suspicions of what was going on in the lord-general's apartments.

Meanwhile by every argument Haslerig and his friends were pressing Monk to take upon himself the civil author-ity as well as the military. It was clear, they said, from the late vote that a restoration was intended, and a res-toration meant his death, for like Stanley, who enthroned the Tudors, he was too great to live. Monk told them to fear nothing. The House merely wanted to leave its successor entirely free, and as for taking upon himself the civil authority, the fate of Cromwell's family was a warning to which he could not be deaf. Haslerig urged that Cromwell was a usurper, while Monk would be acclaimed by the nation. He himself was prepared to bring a petition with a hundred thousand signatures. But the lord-general was obdurate, and dismissing the conspirators he repaired to his place at the Council. The moment he appeared Ashley Cooper got up and moved that the room be cleared and the doors locked.

Then he charged Monk with having received some in-
decent overtures from seditious persons, and demanded a
full disclosure of their nature that the Council might take
steps accordingly. But the kindly old general had no
mind to see proscriptions begin. He had no idea of letting
one party shed the blood of another, and being fully determined to hold the balance true till the nation's wishes
could be weighed, he was not averse to letting the Council
see what volcanic forces he could explode upon them at a
word. "There is not so much danger in agitation as you
apprehend," he said when Ashley Cooper had done. "It
is true some have been with me to be resolved in scruples
concerning the present transactions in Parliament, but
they went away from me well satisfied." And the Council
had to tamely receive the rebuke of the fearless look and
laconic address which their consciences were too guilty
to resent.

So the incident ended, but not without one important
result. As Gumble had lost the general's ear from being
suspected probably of too close an understanding with
his old patron Scot, so now Clarges, who had succeeded
him, was superseded by a new councillor. By the
advice of his brother Nicholas the general invited his
kinsman Morice, the secluded member for Plymouth, to
come up and take his seat, and from this time forward
the slow-witted soldier had at his elbow the political
sagacity of this scholarly recluse.

It was indeed fortunate that he had, for he was not
yet to be left in peace. Haslerig immediately returned
to the attack with a petition from a number of officers
begging the lord-general to sign a declaration in favour
of a Commonwealth and against a single person, and to

get the Parliament to do the same. In the army lay the
great danger to the country. Monk knew that the only
chance of a settlement rested on his ability to keep it in
hand till the great voice of the nation could speak its
mind with overwhelming authority. Sensible of the
gravity of the situation, he told the deputation he would
give them an answer in Council of War on the morrow.
He was confronted with a danger as great as any he had
yet encountered, and he met it with his usual address.
To the malcontents' arguments his spokesmen answered
that their fears and hopes were alike groundless. The
writs ran in the name of the Commonwealth, and every
one who had served against the Parliament was disquali-
fied. In any case no good could come of an attempt to
put pressure on the House, for it would only dissolve
itself and plunge the nation once more into anarchy.
And they need not hope that the lord-general in that
event would assume the government. They would
merely be left a prey to the common enemy. Monk
confirmed all his friends had said in the usual laconic
speech with which he was wont to close such discussions.
Still they were not satisfied. An officer continued to
boldly argue that the qualifications were no safeguard,
as the new Parliament alone had power to decide whether
they had been observed. The argument was unanswer-
able. Monk abruptly cut it short by saying that the
meetings of military councils to meddle with civil
matters were subversive of discipline, and for the future
he absolutely forbade them. The army was still tingling
with the blows by which the terrible disciplinarian had
broken it to his will. In various parts of the country
where insubordination had shown itself new ones had

been inflicted to remind them in whose grip they were.
The new spirit of modern discipline which Monk had
begotten was already arising, and Haslerig was once more
baffled.

Still he was not defeated, and the last hours of the
great Parliament are obscured in the mists of another
intrigue in which the indomitable Republican played a
mysterious part. A resolution had been passed that the
dissolution should take place on or before March 16th.
As the time drew near signs of a strong disinclina-
tion to abide by it began to appear. Monk, who had
retired to St. James's to keep as much in the background
as possible, began to have his suspicions. The original
understanding had been that they were to sit for about
a week and do nothing but arrange for a new Parliament
and an interim Government, and to take measures to keep
the military Fanatics quiet. This merely meant that they
were to provide Monk with pay for the army and all
that was necessary for the preservation of order. They
chose, however, to interpret it by passing a Bill for the
re-establishment of the militia, and putting it into the
hands of their own men. Not content with this breach
of faith, they began busying themselves with Church
matters. In a Presbyterian and Independent Parliament
such questions were not to be settled in an hour. When
the writs came out, moreover, it was found that they had
been made returnable five days later than the specified
time. The Militia Bill had gone to the printers, but had
not yet been published. A committee was sent to inquire
into the delay. It was found that the Bill had been
tampered with in the press. Haslerig was suspected of
being at the bottom of it. However that may be, it had

the effect he would have wished. Monk's suspicions were changed to certainties. At St. James's it became clear that the Presbyterians were manœuvring to gain time, till they had the new militia in readiness to support them in prolonging their sitting and recalling the King on their own terms. Pym indeed had so openly advocated this course that the general had had to send for him privately and warn him to hold his tongue. It was just what Monk had feared, but though his own sympathies were in favour of the moderate Presbyterians, he was not going to allow that party to steal a march on the country any more than the Cavaliers or Fanatics or Republicans, and he put his foot down at once.

When the House met on the 6th an ominous letter from the redoubtable general was in the Speaker's hands. Like naughty children conscious of their guilt, they voted that it should not be opened for the present lest it contained a command for them to be gone. The previous day the Bill for settling Hampton Court upon the general had been thrown out on the third reading, at the instance of his friends, it was said, but from what ensued it would seem that at least it was done with unseemly alacrity; and if Monk did not approve of it, it is certainly strange that it was allowed to proceed so far. At all events, as the alarming letter lay unopened before them, they hurriedly voted the lord-general £20,000 and the stewardship of the palace and all its parks. Then the seal was broken and the general's message read. It assured them that he would be responsible for the peace of the Commonwealth with his army, and desired them to stop the reorganisation of the militia. What more it contained we do not know. The immediate effect was that the House despatched a committee to St. James's to give satisfaction to the irate general, and voted to take the question of dissolution the first thing after dinner.

As soon as the members met again after the mid-day adjournment the committee reported that they had been to the general, and he was satisfied with their explanations. But the House had been taught a lesson, and in a few hours, by its own act, the most renowned Parliament that ever sat was no more.

CHAPTER XIII

MONK had now led the country another distinct march along the thorny path he was clearing with such anxious devotion, and Sir William Davenant burst out into a long panegyric on the occasion. But at the same time he reminded the general—

> " Yet greater work ensues such as will try
> How far three realms may on your strength rely."

The Parliament was gone, but the Council of State remained, and there the patriotic struggle began again ! The Presbyterian section was strong, and outside it was backed by a powerful combination, at the head of which were Northumberland, Manchester and the men of the days to which the Self-Denying Ordinance put an end. These saw that a restoration was inevitable, and felt that the only salvation of the country lay in a renewal of the Isle of Wight treaty. Though baulked by Monk's watchfulness in their attempt to get the King recalled by a Presbyterian Parliament, they did not despair of outmarching the Cavaliers and Opportunists. Their last chance was in a restoration through the agency of the Council of State before the new Parliament could meet, and again and again they pressed Monk to openly espouse their

cause. He only said he was in the service of the Commonwealth and could not listen. The pressure grew greater,
the party more powerful, and he found it necessary to
treat their proposals more seriously, but still he gave no
hope. In despair, at last, they seized upon some expression he had let fall to send word to the King that they had
won him, and that they were prepared to enter into formal negotiations for a restoration. A fortnight before
the needy voluptuary, weary of his exile, would have
embraced the offer with avidity, but now, to the astonishment of all concerned, the proposition was coldly, almost contemptuously received. Something had happened
of which they were in entire ignorance, something so
singular as almost to startle us anew into an exaggeration
of the personal influence in history.

Up till now Monk's reputation as a Commonwealth
man was practically without a spot. By honestly doing
his duty he had lived down every suspicion. All but
the most sanguine of the Cavalier agents considered him
hopelessly loyal to his trust. Best known of these was
his cousin Sir John Grenville, who, in spite of his notorious malignancy, was free of St. James's on the ground of
his relationship. But he had no better luck than the
rest. Fruitlessly he sought a private interview through
his old friend Morice. Night after night he stayed till
every one was gone, but "Good-night, cousin; 'tis late,"
was all he got for his pains as the wary old general went
off to bed.

Such was Monk's position when the Portuguese ambassador asked for an audience. The recent treaty of the
Pyrenees had left Portugal at the mercy of Spain, and
she had sent a special envoy to England to seek assistance.

For some time past the envoy had been in negotiation
with the Council of State for a renewal of Cromwell's
alliance, but the action of the Presbyterian leaders seems
to have demonstrated to him that its authority was
moribund. The power of Monk and the now inevitable
recall of the King suggested to him a brilliant piece of
diplomacy, and he resolved to flash a dazzling proposal in
the eyes of the general. Father Russell, the secretary
to the embassy, seems first to have sounded Morice. But
at all events, amidst the enormous mass of business with
which he exhausted his secretaries, Monk found time for
an interview.

The ambassador began by saying that without wish-
ing to pry into the general's intentions with regard to
the King, he thought it only right to tell him that Charles
Stuart ought at once to get out of Spanish territory.
He was then at Brussels, and the envoy assured Monk
that the moment the Spaniards got wind of the national
reaction in favour of a restoration they would kidnap his
person, and hold him as a hostage for the retrocession of
Jamaica and Dunkirk. Monk, who already had reason
to suspect the Spaniards of intriguing with the Irreconcilables through the Jesuits, was much impressed, and the
ambassador was encouraged to explain his solicitude for
Charles's safety. In the event of a restoration, he said,
his master was prepared, in return for military assistance
against Spain, to offer the King the hand of the Infanta,
and with her a dowry of an unheard-of sum of money,
together with the towns of Tangiers and Bombay. The
advantages of the arrangement it was needless to point
out. It would give to England the command of the
Mediterranean and East Indian trade, and enable her to

complete the humiliation of her great rival which the heroes of the Armada had begun.

To a man of Monk's hot patriotism, who remembered Raleigh, who had been moulded into manhood while Drake and Grenville and Hawkins were living memories, the proposal was too dazzling to resist. His passion for the expansion of England had never been quenched. His faith in it as a panacea for all political trouble was as strong as ever. Before him stretched the prospect of a glorious war, in which the fierce ardour of the Fanatic soldiers would find worthy employ, and serve to lift their country out of the slough into which they had plunged it to a greatness beyond the dreams of their fathers. The fires of his youth were rekindled. He may even have dreamed of ending his career in wiping out the disgrace in which it had begun, and at the head of the most powerful navy and the finest army in the world of outshining the greatest of the great Queen's captains.

Whatever was the overmastering cause, the wary strategist suddenly changed front, cast his scruples to the winds, and the Portuguese ambassador immediately applied to the Council for a frigate to carry him and his portentous secret to Lisbon. Monk had determined to communicate with the King. Charles's danger was great and pressing. At any moment a precipitate message from the Presbyterians to the Court might give the Spaniard the signal to act; nor was the anxious general without good ground to suspect that the French ambassador was intriguing with the Manchester cabal, and that Mazarin had a chance, if not an intention, of playing the same game. On the eve of its accomplishment the long-wished-for settlement was in desperate peril of

wreck, and calm and swift as ever the old soldier set to
work single-handed to thwart the designs of the two
most renowned diplomatists in Europe.

Absolute secrecy was essential. The Portuguese
negotiations with the Committee of Safety were continued as if nothing had happened, and the general
looked round for a messenger on whom he could implicitly rely. Morice could not be spared, and it was
clear that Grenville was the only man. After two
ineffectual attempts to induce him to disclose his secret
mission to Morice, Monk was convinced of his discretion,
and granted him an interview. In the dead of night,
shortly after the dissolution, he was introduced into
Morice's private apartments at St. James's. The general
appeared from a secret stairway, and Grenville without
preface or apology thrust into his hands the King's
letters which his cousin Nicholas had refused to take up
to Scotland. Monk started back, and asked him fiercely
how he dared so play the traitor.

The Cavalier quietly replied that in the service
of the King, his master, danger had grown familiar
to him. Overcome with his young kinsman's coolness,
and the memories of all he owed to his house, the
old general unbent at once and cordially embraced him.
Then he read the King's letter. In flattering terms
it assured him of Charles's favour, and of his intention to
follow Monk's advice implicitly if he would only espouse
his cause. Grenville added what he had been authorised
to promise—a hundred thousand a year for him and
his officers, any title he chose, and the office of Lord
High Constable. Monk replied that what he did was
for his country's good, and that he would not sell

his duty or bargain for his allegiance. Grenville pressed for a written answer, but the wary soldier refused; he had intercepted too many letters himself. Grenville was told he must take his reply by word of mouth, and so was dismissed till the morrow.

For some time past the general had had confidential consultations with the leaders of the various parties, with a view apparently of finding a common ground on which a settlement might be made when the new Parliament met. Lenthal, for whose ripe experience Monk seems to have had a high regard, had suggested as the terms that would be most satisfactory to the country, a general amnesty, the confirmation of the land-titles, and liberty of conscience. These the general now determined to make the basis of negotiation, and when Grenville returned the following evening he found them incorporated in a pithy memorandum. An urgent appeal to the King to leave Brussels for some place in Holland was added, and a strict caution to Grenville that he was not to ask for any reward for the service Monk was doing. After reading over these instructions to his cousin several times till he had them by heart, the general threw the paper into the fire. With final orders not to leave Charles till he was out of Spanish territory, and not even to treat of a reward, Grenville was dismissed, and left London the same night. Thus it was that when the letter of the Presbyterians surprised the exultant exiles in the act of preparing an answer to the general's message of salvation, the King only laughed, and said, "I perceive that these people do not know that I and General Monk stand on much better terms."

Charles at once acted on the general's advice, and after seeing him safely upon Dutch soil, Grenville on April 4th hastened back with a dangerous burden. Besides official letters for the two Houses of Parliament, the Council, the army, and the city, each containing a copy of the famous Declaration from Breda, he carried an autograph letter from the King to the general, together with a commission for him to be Captain-General of the Three Kingdoms, and a signet and seal for a Secretary of State, to be delivered to whomsoever the general chose. The letter Monk accepted, but he had still enough of the true soldier of fortune in him to refuse a commission incompatible with the one he held. Nor would he take the seals, but told Grenville to hide himself and his papers till Parliament met, and then act according to his instructions.

The few Royalists who were in the secret were already in a state of ecstasy. Mordaunt, who had been working successfully in other quarters, had written over that nothing could now stop the King's return but an attempt by Lambert on the Council or Monk. Fortunately Lambert was in the Tower, but nevertheless the danger was great. As the designs of the Presbyterians became known the army grew more and more restless. Agitators began to persuade them they were to be cheated out of land, arrears, and all the long struggle had won them. Monk saw his regiments must be still further purged. To effect this Charles Howard of Naworth, who commanded his bodyguard, together with Ashley Cooper and the old Coldstreamers, prepared a petition to him that every officer should be required, in view of the insubordinate spirit that was arising, to sign an engagement to be true to the Government as it was then constituted. The precaution was taken none too soon. A few days after Grenville's return a letter was intercepted disclosing a conspiracy of Anarchists and extreme Republicans as formidable as any with which Cromwell had had to contend. It was written from Wales by Desborough, the most formidable of the Fanatics, to a partisan in the city. The idea involved the destruction of Charles and his brothers as well as of Monk, and early in May the Fanatics were to rise in Wales, seize all the towns on the Marches, and set up the Long Parliament at Shrewsbury. By this masterly move they hoped to attract the Presbyterians, whom they had been careful to make jealous of the Cavaliers. Already it appeared they had the support of the Jesuits, who, as Monk knew very well, were always ready to join hands with Independency. Till all was ready the army was to be kept in a state of ferment and distrust of its leaders, and the new House was to have "bones to pick," so as to prevent the possibility of any decided step being taken towards the King's recall. Vane was to lead the insurrection, and Haslerig's support was expected. Already the city had quarrelled with the Presbyterian leaders. Other signs of the conspirators' work appeared, and Monk and the Council were taking their precautions when suddenly the danger was doubled. On April 11th (or 10th), after Colonel Howard had presented the officers' petition to the general, like a thunderclap came the news that Lambert had escaped from the Tower.

It was at such a moment that Monk was greatest. Small as was his opinion of his rival as a soldier, he knew

Lambert was looked upon by the malcontents of the army as their champion. It was a name to conjure with, and the Fanatics had got the one thing wanting, a man the soldiers would follow. Monk acted with all his old energy. Arrests were made right and left. The new Engagement was presented to all the regiments, and every officer who refused to sign was cashiered. Morgan was reinforced in Scotland and the city militia mobilised. Still the work had only begun. Lambert, after narrowly escaping arrest in the city, got away into the country. The expected desertions began, and Monk ordered the Engagement to be signed by rank and file as well as officers. Whole troops and companies refused, and whole troops and companies were disarmed and broken. As fast as one regiment was sound it was despatched to remodel another; but hardly was the operation complete than intelligence came that Lambert had appeared in arms in the western Midlands. Instantly Colonels Howard and Ingoldsby—daring Dick Ingoldsby, Cromwell's favourite *sabreur*, "who could neither pray nor preach"—were hurried with two flying columns to the scene of action; but that was not all. Monk was not a man to do things by halves. The events of the next week it was impossible to foretell; he could only prepare for the worst. By the elections the country had already declared for the King, and, determined at all costs to save it from Lambert and the Fanatics, Monk sent for Sir John Grenville. He told him that if the rising were not immediately crushed the army might revolt at any time. "In that case," he continued, "I shall publish my commission from the King, and raise all the royal party of the three nations." Sir John was instructed to hold

himself in readiness to convey the necessary orders to the
leading Cavaliers, and that night his brother Barnard
was speeding towards Holland with the general's warning
to the King.

Monk's heroic remedy was destined to be untried.
His energy had once more saved the country from civil
war. On Easter Tuesday, six days after the alarm was
given, a grand review of the mobilised trained-bands was
held in Hyde Park. From ten thousand throats the
great Royalist reaction found voice. Many cheered for
the King openly; the auxiliaries drank his health on their
knees ; George Monk was the darling of the hour. As
though nothing should be wanting from his triumph,
when the enthusiasm was at its highest a party of
travel-stained horse was seen moving along the outskirts
of the park. Right under the gallows at Tyburn they
passed, and a new shout rent the air ; for in their midst
rode Lambert with swordless scabbard.

His attempt was premature, and had been crushed at
a blow. Pistol in hand, Dick Ingoldsby had ridden him
down as he galloped from the field ; but the great conspiracy was practically untouched. Desborough's agents
redoubled their activity. Monk's officers, sensible of the
danger, came to beg him to proclaim the King at once
before Parliament met, and so win the whole glory for
himself and the army. But even the stirring scene
in the park could not shake his splendid self-control.
He quietly reminded them of their oft-expressed determination to keep the military power in obedience to the
civil, and of the Engagement they had so recently signed.
What they proposed, he said, was treason, and so he
dismissed them.

In spite of the danger which still threatened from the
Parliamentary delays, which he knew the Fanatics were
fostering, he was determined to proceed in a constitutional
manner, and he arranged with his cousin, Charles's ac-
credited agent, the exact method of procedure.   Parliament met quietly on the 25th.   Monk took his seat
for Devon, having elected to sit for his native county
in preference to Cambridge University by which he had
been also returned.   The Commons next day passed the
general a vote of thanks for his unparalleled services in
having conquered the enemies of Church and State without so much as "a bloody nose."   The few Presbyterian
Lords who had met uninvited and unresisted did the same,
and Monk in his acknowledgment bluntly begged them
to look forward and not backward in transacting affairs,
a hint they were careful to take.   While this was going
on in Parliament Sir John Grenville presented himself at
the Council-chamber and asked to see the lord-general.
Monk came out and received from his cousin's hands as
from a stranger an official letter addressed "To our trusty
and well-beloved General Monk, to be by him communicated to the President and Council of State, and to the
officers of the armies under his command."   Monk at once
ordered his guards to detain the messenger and returned
to the Council-chamber.   There he broke the seal and
handed the letter unread to the president.   The surprise
was complete.   No one but Morice had an idea of what
had been going on.   Still it was clear that the letter
came from Charles, and after some debate it was resolved
that without being read it should be presented to Parliament on May 1st, the day they had fixed for the business of the settlement of the nation.   Meanwhile

Grenville was to be placed under arrest, but the general interposed, saying that although a stranger he was a near kinsman of his own, and that he would be responsible for his appearance at the bar.

But it was not intended that Grenville should wait for the summons. So soon as the Houses met he attended, and sprung upon them the official letters he had for each. In the Commons Morice was on his feet before the House could recover its breath, and moved that the constitutional government of the country was by King, Lords, and Commons. The motion was carried in a rush of enthusiasm, and Monk asked leave to communicate the King's despatch to the army. It was granted. Similar votes were passed in the Lords, and the Commonwealth was constitutionally at an end. At a subsequent sitting, however, the House came a little more to its senses. Sir Matthew Hale rose to move for a committee to inquire what terms had been offered to the late King. Monk saw, or thought he saw, the cloven hoof of the Sectaries. Here was one of the "bones to pick" which he knew they meant to provide. He rose to his feet immediately and solemnly warned the House not to presume on the apparent quiet of the country. Incendiaries, he said, were on the watch for a place to raise a flame : he had full information, which it was not expedient to make public ; but he could not answer for the army or undertake to preserve order if the King were not sent for at once. There is no reason to doubt not only that he believed what he said, but that it was really true, and that the Sectaries and Republicans were fast loosening his grip on the troops. Relying on Charles's promises to himself, he saw no danger in his

unconditional return, for, as he went on to point out
to the House, without troops or money the King would
be at their mercy. He concluded by moving that commissioners should be immediately sent to invite Charles to
England; "And the blood be on the head of him," he
cried, "who delays the settlement."[1]

His words were greeted with a thunder of applause.
The old constitutionalists saw that Monk's appeal was
irresistible, and in the excitement of the moment vote
after vote was passed that went beyond the most extravagant hopes of the most sanguine Cavalier. The Revolution was at an end, and the lord-general's lady proceeded
to herald the new era by frankly turning to her old trade
and purchasing a stock of linen at wholesale prices on
the King's account for Whitehall.

The rapid transformation that followed is a matter of
history. Both France and Spain saw the victim of their
long intrigues suddenly snatched from their grasp, and
each made desperate efforts to coax him back into its
power. All their blandishments were in vain. Monk
had succeeded in his resolve that if the King came back
it should be without entangling the country in any engagements with foreign powers. Mazarin and De Haro
had been completely outwitted by the dull soldier, and
the cardinal died of vexation, it used to be said, in the
following year.

Early on May 25th Monk was roused at Canterbury with the news that the fleet, which was bringing

---

[1] Burnet, i. p. 88. There is no trace of Hale's motion in the
Journals, but it may have been purposely omitted. Mordaunt in
his letter to the king on May 4th seems to be ignorant of what Monk
had done, *Clar. S. P.* iii.

home the King, was in sight. There he had just arrived,
the idol of the swarms of gentlemen that were flocking to
Dover to welcome Charles and push their fortunes. He
was worshipped and tormented as the fountain of honour.
In his pocket he had a long list of importunate friends
and enemies whom he had good-naturedly promised to
recommend for places in the Government. His bodyguard
was filled with noblemen. The very roads threatened to
be blocked with the multitude of high-born supplicants,
till the old disciplinarian, shocked at the indecency of the
scramble, imperiously enrolled them into regiments and
insisted on some order being observed.

Monk was "the sole pillar of the King's confidence,"
and so soon as the fleet reached Dover Roads Charles
sent an express to say that he would not land till he
came to him. No sooner was the summons received than
he was on horseback again hastening to Dover. The
critical moment had come. Every one then agreed that
it was Monk who had restored the King, but how and why
no one could exactly tell. As the boat containing the
royal party touched the beach they crowded round to see
the meeting of the two uncrowned kings, hoping that
Monk's demeanour would lift the mist in which the future
was wrapped and show them who was going to wield the
sceptre. Charles himself was as nervous and anxious as
the rest. This formidable figure that had arisen so
suddenly and with such mystery, this man of darkness
who had done as it were single-handed what for years
had defied the efforts of his own most trusted councillors,
and who yet forbade the very mention of reward, the
perplexed King could only fear.

On the beach they met, and to every one's surprise the

soldierly figure sank upon its knee and kissed the royal hand as deferentially as though it were the king who had made the general. Startled into an unwonted display of emotion Charles raised him, and embracing him with genuine fervour called him his father. Both were too moved for many words. Without more ado, amidst the shouts of the people and the thunder of the guns from forts and fleet, the two walked side by side to the royal coach. There the soldier of fortune took his place with the King and his brothers; and the Duke of Buckingham was clever enough, to every one's annoyance, to get possession of the boot uninvited.

The transports of delight which marked the whole progress to Canterbury were like a dream to Charles, so little could he understand it all. His first sensation, when he had time to realise his position quietly, was one of disgust at the indecency with which petitions for places had been showered upon him the moment he landed. It was impossible to satisfy them all, and the throne before him bid fair to be a bed of thorns; but far worse was yet to come. Hardly was he alone when the terrible general came into his room. Monk was no courtier, and his Court manners were already exhausted. It was a visit of business, and his way of doing business was aggressively direct. Without any preface or apology he went straight to the point, and in his blunt rough way told the King he could not do him better service than to recommend him councillors who would be acceptable to the people. With that he handed in his list of names. Charles nervously thrust it into his pocket, thanked the general, and dismissed him. Clarendon was sent for, and together they read the alarming memorandum. It contained the

names of but two Cavaliers. Charles was aghast. What
did it mean? Was this the solution of Monk's extraordinary conduct? Did he intend to be mayor of the
palace to a *roi fainéant?* Clarendon knew as well as
Monk the great revolutionary forces that were straining
unseen beneath all the enthusiasm. He knew they were
only kept under by an army which sympathised with
them in its heart. The fleet was still riding off Dover;
Monk had only to hold up his finger, and in a few hours
the King would be on his travels again. The chancellor
determined to get Morice to find out what the general
intended. In an hour he came back. The general, he
reported, was extremely pained that he had caused the
King any uneasiness. He held the royal commission,
and was there to receive orders, not to give them. The
paper was merely a list of persons he had promised to
recommend. The King was at perfect liberty to accept
or reject them, only there were a few whom he heartily
wished he could make use of.

The episode was ended; the King breathed again, but
he never forgot the fright. Till the veteran passed away
Charles never ceased to fear his power and love the hand
that used him so gently. Ashley Cooper, whom Monk
specially recommended, was sworn a Privy Councillor on
the spot, together with the general himself, Morice, and
the Earl of Southampton; but the King committed himself no further. Morice was also given the seals which
Monk had refused to confer in spite of a heavy bribe,
and the general himself received the Garter at the hands
of the Dukes of York and Gloucester. He was offered
the choice of any of the great offices of State, and he
characteristically chose that of Master of the Horse. It

had little or nothing to do with politics, and the patronage was extensive.

So the play was ended, and in a blaze of triumph such as England had never known the King entered London in the midst of a magnificent procession. Immediately behind him rode the lord-general beside the obtrusive Duke of Buckingham. Never before or since has a subject occupied such a position and arrogated less to himself. The ovation with which the King and his deliverer were received was deafening. Charles was perfectly dazed. He could hardly speak to his faithful Parliament as Lords and Commons met him jostling one another in a disorderly and excited mob. He recognised no one, and was so exhausted with the din that he could not attend the Thanksgiving in the Abbey. So as though the note of incapacity must be struck at the outset, he turned aside and took refuge in Whitehall. Still the glory of the conqueror was none the less, nor his satisfaction less complete. He could lay his head on his pillow that night with the happy consciousness that the burden of empire was lifted from his shoulders, that his country was at peace again, and still more, which was dearest of all to his great heart, that the triumph had been won without the cost of a single life.

CHAPTER XIV

To follow Monk's career after the Restoration in detail would here be out of place. It adds but little to our knowledge of the man and labours under the ban of anti-climax. To the student of history and government it is full of interest, yet so unobtrusive was his work that it is now hard to trace beneath the shifting strife of politicians. When men asked what after all this dull work-day soldier had done that the country should idolise him as it did, Secretary Nicholas, who knew, was wont to say that even if he had not put Charles upon his throne, he would still have deserved all the bounties the King had bestowed upon him for his services after the Restoration.

It is a remark profoundly true. His finest work goes unrecorded. To suppose that the whole nation acquiesced at once in the Restoration is almost as great an error as to think that it was conquered by William at Hastings. As yet Monk had but stolen a march on the Irreconcilables. Numbers of ardent spirits belonging to the Anabaptists, the Fifth Monarchy men, and the fighting section of the Quakers, together with a large body of extreme

Independents and Presbyterians, were only waiting for an
opportunity to tear the arch-malignant from his throne
again.   They comprised all the fiery earnestness of the
nation, they breathed the exaggerated spirit of all that has
made us what we are ; and when we see Mrs. Hutchinson
at her heroic colonel's side as he lay rotting in a living
grave; when we think of Harrison's wife buying his blood-
stained clothes of the executioner, and, unable to believe
that God had suffered her saint to die with his work un-
ended, watching over them till he should come again,
—the heart of Monk's profoundest admirer must bleed
that they fell under such a hand as his.

And the kindly heart of the old general bled for
them, too.   Of all the libels that pursued him from the
mouths of those who envied him the royal favour,
or suffered from the success of his patriotic policy, none
is greater than that which accused him of betraying his
friends and persecuting his enemies.   Neither one nor
the other is true.   From the moment his victory was
assured he busied himself unflinchingly in saving the
vanquished from the hands of those who mistook ani-
mosity for zeal.   It was he who cried "Hold !" when
the Convention tried to enlarge the list of exceptions to
the amnesty ; it was he who stayed the vengeance of
the Cavalier Parliament by coming down to the House
with the words of the King in his mouth.   Privately he
worked as nobly.   Numbers of men were preserved upon
some evidence the general had in their favour.   Lambert,
Fleetwood, Lenthal, Milton, and the Cromwells all found
in him a friend at Court.   Haslerig's fears he had laughed
away with a promise to save him for twopence.   His
persistent opponent got off scot free, and the letter is

still extant in which the twopence was sent.[1] Most
wanton of all are those who accuse him of indecency
in sitting on the Regicide Commission, forgetting that
the man who knew enough to hang half the kingdom
could only escape from the witness-box by a seat on the
bench. It were better to remember that he sat there
with seven other adherents of the Revolution of every
shade of opinion, and to credit the King with a desire to
make the commission a representative one, and Monk
with the intention of seeing fair play to the men who
were down.

The darkest cloud upon his memory is his alleged
conduct in reference to Argyle's trial. The charge
against him is that, when the evidence proved incon-
clusive, Monk produced some private correspondence
upon which the marquis was immediately convicted.
The story has hitherto rested on the testimony of
Burnet, a notorious libeller of the general's, and Baillie,
who, like the rest of the Presbyterians, could never
forgive him for foiling their attempt to force upon
the country a covenanted King.   No evidence could be
more tainted, and it is not surprising that the story has
always been doubted, seeing how inconsistent it is with
the character of a man "who could not hate an
enemy beyond the necessity of war." Injudicious
advocates have even denied the fact altogether, but
a bundle of Argyle's letters, including some to Monk
and one to his secretary, was certainly produced at
the last moment, and at once sealed the prisoner's fate.
In consequence of Charles's resolution not to go behind

---

[1] In *Egerton MSS.*, 2618, p. 71. Cf. *Hist. MSS. Rep. V.*, p. 149,
and ii. p. 79 ; Broderick to Hyde, 7th May 1660, *Clar. S. P.*

the Scotch amnesty of 1651, the chief point in Argyle's indictment was that he had adhered to the King's enemies, or, in other words, that he had opposed the last Highland insurrection. The leaders of it were at once his judges and his prosecutors, and they were determined to have their revenge. The case closed and still there was no real evidence, when just as the Court was deliberating its judgment a messenger thundered at the door with the fatal packet from London. Regardless of all law the case was reopened, the letters read, and Argyle condemned.

The question of Monk's share in the infamous proceeding rests on the contents of those letters. They have now been found, and they acquit him for ever. Only two are to him, and they contain no evidence whatever beyond what had been already obtained in abundance. They are confined to little more than civilities. The one to Clarke, Monk's secretary, encloses a letter from Glencairn, and expresses Argyle's intention of keeping his own country neutral. The other three are to Lilburne, and they prove in the clearest manner that Argyle was not only giving the English general information of the Royalist movements, but was doing his best to prevent assistance going to the insurgents.[1] These three letters are not endorsed as having been "admitted" by the prisoner, and could any doubt remain that it was these on which he was convicted, it would be removed by the subsequent petition of Archibald the tenth Earl. For in that

[1] Lord Garden says they were from Deane, but this must be a mistake. See his letter to Stirling of Keir, May 24th, 1661, *Maxwell MSS.*, 68, *Hist. MSS. Rep. X.*, i. p. 74.

document he recites that the fatal letters bore no
"signature" that the marquis "had owned them."
The letters to Monk and Clarke are all endorsed with
Argyle's admission.[1]

Thus we may finally dismiss this wholly uncorrobor-
ated libel about deliberately producing confidential
letters. The compromising documents are State Papers.
That Monk knew enough to cost Argyle his life ten
times over is certain. It is equally certain that he did
not tell what he knew. The tardy production of the
documents and the official nature of their contents
point to the natural explanation of their appearance—a
last despairing search in the archives of the Council of
State by the men who were thirsting for the great
Covenanter's blood, and hungering for his estates.

The libel has not even the excuse of provocation.
Monk did not desert the Presbyterians. He never,
indeed, belonged to their party. He professed their
ecclesiastical opinions, but never embraced their political
creed. Nor did he fail to stand by them in the hour of
need. For not only did he give the leaders certificates
of their services to the Restoration, but when it was
found impossible to prevent the passing of the Bill of
Uniformity, the "man that was all made of mercy"
joined with his old political opponent Lord Manchester
in urging the King not to enforce it in all its rigour.
Nor did Charles finally make surrender to the persecuting spirit of the Anglican majority in Parliament till
Monk was lying in state.

Still it is not to be wondered at that such stories
pursued him. The very loftiness of his station was

[1] See *Argyle MSS.*, 80-85, *Hist. MSS. Rep. VI.*, p. 617.

enough to breed them in men less fortunate. Besides his Garter, his Mastership of the Horse, and his exalted commission, he was raised to the peerage by the title of Duke of Albemarle, Earl of Torrington, and Baron Monk of Potheridge, Beauchamp, and Tees. For a while he was also Lord Lieutenant of Ireland. He was made a gentleman of the Bedchamber, and as though that did not place him near enough to the person of the grateful King, by his patent as Captain-General he was granted the extraordinary privilege of entering the presence at any hour unannounced, and remaining there till he was told to go. The King never ceased to treat him as a father. Indeed Charles's unswerving devotion to his deliverer is enough to redeem his character from the sweeping charge of baseness that is sometimes made against it. As a member of the inner committee of the Privy Council, the parent of all cabinets, Monk must have constantly had to lecture and thwart his master, but never once did he give a sign that the old duke's favour was declining.

By the King he was regarded as a father, and by the country as no less. "The body of the people," said the Bishop of Exeter in his funeral sermon, "loved and honoured him, nay (God forgive them), they believed and trusted in him." There was never an awkward job to be done, or failure to be rectified, or panic to be allayed, but the Duke of Albemarle was sent for like an old family doctor. Was there a powerful minister to be dismissed, the Duke had to break the news to him ; the Treasury accounts got into confusion, and the Duke was put on to the commission to set them straight ; the plague drove Court and Parliament

from the capital, and he was left behind sitting in
Whitehall with his life in his hand, seeing every one
who presented himself day after day at a time when
brother would hardly speak to brother, or husband
to wife, and through the whole of that terrible period
he managed in his own person army, navy, treasury,
and police.   The Duke of York failed as an admiral,
and " old George" was asked if he would mind taking
command.   The great fire destroyed half London, and
threw the country into a panic, and the King, in terror
of a new revolution, had to beg "the sole pillar of
the state" to come up from the fleet and restore
confidence.   The people openly said it never would
have happened if the general had been there; and
when the Dutch sailed into the Thames men seemed
to think he had only to go down to Chatham for the
enemy to scatter like chaff.

As the country recovered from its fever of royalism,
and began to look back first without disgust, then with
regret to the days of Oliver, it saw in the Protector's
old general the personification of all the glories of the
Commonwealth.   He stood out in startling contrast to
the butterfly throng amongst whom he had his place, and
the courtiers felt it.   Every one laughed at the stupid old
soldier for his homeliness, his mean establishment, his
vulgar wife, and the dulness and lethargy which grew
on him with his disease.   But every one feared him also.
Every request he pressed was granted as a matter of
course.   Even the King did not dare or care to give him
a command, but always sounded him through Morice to
ascertain whether he were willing to do what was wanted.

To detail his endless services is here impossible.   His

greatest work was undoubtedly the disbanding of the great revolutionary army. Some sixty thousand men had to be loosed upon a country seething with the fanatical opinions which the army had made its own, and of which, in spite of Monk's purging, it still was full. Statesmen knew it was the great danger the restored monarchy had to face. To Monk the task was committed; and he did it not only peaceably, but so well that the disbanded soldiers, instead of being so many germs of disaffection, earned themselves, through the facilities the general was careful to provide for their employment, the reputation of being the best citizens in the State.

Another debt which the nation owed to George Monk, whether for good or ill it is hard to say, was entirely due to the confidence his unblemished career had inspired. The Revolution had taken fire in the heat of a quarrel as to which estate of the realm was to control the army. That that dispute did not recur to mar the harmony of the Restoration, and even to render it impossible, was due to the simple fact that the nation trusted "honest George." As soon as it was known that he held the royal commission of Captain-General not a word was uttered on the question. In his hands the country knew that it was safe.

Thus it was that he became the Father of the British Army. It was he who, in the few regiments that were kept on foot to overawe the Sectaries, started its glorious traditions. It was he who gave it its unequalled note of duty and devotion. It was he who once and for ever pronounced that it must be a thing apart from politics, and taught it that a soldier's greatest glory is to obey. In every characteristic of which it is proudest, or for

which we love it best, glitters the stamp of its first commander's personality. Whether we see its officers rising
in the hour of peril above the personal jealousies which
have ruined so many of our neighbours' enterprises, or
admire its dogged obstinacy, its cheerful discipline, and
its chivalrous impatience of party strife ; or whether we
glory in the strange contempt it has ever shown for its
enemies, making a pastime of war,—we have but to turn to
see each finest trait reflected as in a mirror in the life of
the man who gave it breath.   Strange, indeed, it is that
a body in which *esprit de corps* has reached its noblest
development should have forgotten as it has the hero
who begot it, and guided its first halting steps along the
splendid path it was to tread.

    And yet the cause is plain enough.   Like the rest of
the great characters of the English Revolution, Monk has
till recently been only visible through the literature of
the Restoration.   The navy was then the fashion, and
Monk was only known to the historians of the time as an
admiral.   That aspect of him obscured every other.
Society patronised the navy ; it even divided itself into
two cliques on the subject, the partisans of the general
and the partisans of Lord Sandwich.   Montague's party
included nearly all the Court, and unfortunately his two
talented placemen Pepys and Evelyn, whose testimony
wherever their patron's rival is concerned is so tainted
with gratitude as to be almost worthless.   Yet from them
he is chiefly judged, though they manifestly will never
say a good word for him if they can help it; and the Clerk
of the Check at least is never more happy than when he
is pouring lively contempt upon his seamanship, his
duchess, and his dinners.

Monk, however, was secure in the favour of the King and the nation, and, as has been said, it was to him they turned in their trouble after the unsatisfactory naval campaign of 1665. The two admirals had come out of it far from well. Both the Duke of York and Lord Sandwich were accused of cowardice, and Monk had charged his rival with something very like embezzling prize-money. In recognition of their services the prince was told he could not be allowed to expose his life again, and the peer was sent out of the way as ambassador to Madrid. It was, in fact, resolved to supersede them by Prince Rupert and the lord-general. The only question was, would the great man condescend to accept the appointment? After sounding Morice the King with considerable trepidation determined to try. In the autumn Monk was suddenly summoned to Oxford from his post of danger at Whitehall, which with heroic devotion he had never left since the plague broke out. In three days he was back again, and with a throb of delight the country heard that the Duke of Albemarle was to command the fleet next year. Though longing for rest and enfeebled with disease, he had accepted the divided command without a murmur. The only condition he made was that his wife should not know of it till the last moment, for he was sure she would be furious with him for going to sea again. But the appointment was too popular to be kept a secret. The country was confident that nothing could withstand the Duke of Albemarle. The news spread like fire, and the fond old general had some bad half-hours before he sailed in the spring.

On June 1st, while separated from Rupert, he met the Dutch fleet under De Ruyter, outnumbering him nearly two to one. A council of war was called, but the old general's antipathy for cowardice had grown to be almost a monomania. He "hated a coward as ill as a toad," and every officer there knew that the barest suggestion that savoured of prudence would cost him his ship. Of course he attacked, and against such an enemy the issue was a foregone conclusion. After a three days' fight his fleet was cut to pieces. The wonder is that it was not annihilated. It was only by a brilliant display of all his old mastery of naval tactics that he got its shattered remains into the Thames.[1]

On the evening of the third day Rupert joined him, and on the morrow he staggered out once more in the prince's company. Astonished as the Dutch had been at the reckless daring of Monk with his fleet of wrecks, they thought it impossible for him again to put to sea, and had gone back to Holland to refit. About eight o'clock they were sighted to windward, and at once fell into line and lay to to wait for the English. Monk was for attacking immediately. Up till now he had modestly given way to Rupert's greater nautical experience, but now the prince wanted to slacken sail to let the Blue division close up as it was far astern. Monk flew into a passion, but as even he could not call the daring prince a coward, he had reluctantly to admit that he

[1] The statement that this action was fought without order rests on a remark which Pepys said was made to him by Penn. Penn had quarrelled with Monk, who was the terror of his party, and he was not present at the action. Jordan wrote him an account of it, but his letter gives the impression of a line carefully following the movements of the admiral (Penn's *Life*, ii. p. 389 ; *Gumble*, p. 423), and this is confirmed by the official account which gives in detail the whole of Monk's elaborate manœuvres, *S. P. Dom.* clviii. f. 46.

was prudent. While the gay young Duke of Buckingham, who, not to be out of the fashion, had joined the fleet as a volunteer, was laughing to see Rupert for once in his life on the side of caution, the furious old general was caught quietly loading a little pocket-pistol. It was a curious weapon for a sea-fight, and Monk had been heard to say that whatever happened he did not mean to be taken. It could only be intended to blow up the ship as a last resource. "And therefore," says Buckingham, "Mr. Saville and I in a laughing way most mutinously resolved to throw him overboard in case we should ever find him going down to the powder-room."

The action which ensued was indecisive, but the advantage on the four days was certainly with the Dutch. Still the old general would never admit it. He always maintained he had inflicted greater loss on De Ruyter than he had suffered himself. He did not dream he was beaten. He accused the greater part of his officers, certainly with some reason, of cowardice, and even of treachery. Not above twenty of them, he used to say, had behaved like men ; and in unshaken contempt of his brave enemy he set to work desperately to refit and begin again more furious and confident than ever.

The Dutch were out first, and lay in triumph in the mouth of the Thames with a hundred sail. By incredible exertions Monk and Rupert had a like number ready before the end of July, and dropped down the river to meet the enemy. The Dutch retired to their own coasts and the English gave chase. Early on the morning of the 25th the enemy were sighted to leeward. They at once took the crescent formation to await the attack. The English came on in grand order. Every ship took up its

position in splendid style, and by ten o'clock the whole
line was hotly engaged. Monk and Rupert on the *Royal
Charles*, formerly the *Naseby*, singled out De Ruyter, but
even the boldness with which the Dutch admiral accepted
the engagement could not in the least reduce Monk's
contempt. The old general stood unmoved on the
quarter-deck chewing his tobacco as the Dutch flagship
ranged alongside. "Now," said he, "will this fellow
come and give me two broadsides, and then he shall run."
Two broadsides were exchanged, but De Ruyter did not
run, nor yet at the third or fourth. For two hours the
kings of the fleets fought hand to hand in Homeric
strife, till the *Royal Charles* was a perfect wreck aloft and
had to fall astern. "Methinks, sir," said an officer to
the Duke, "De Ruyter hath given us more than two
broadsides." The old soldier only turned his quid to say,
"Well, but you shall find him run by and by." And so
he did at last. Jordan had taken the generals' place, and
in half an hour they had bent new tackle enough to
engage again. But before De Ruyter gave way he had
once more reduced the *Royal Charles* to such a state that
her boats had to tow her out of the line and the generals
shifted their flags to the *Royal James*.

De Ruyter brought off his shattered fleet in such
masterly style that little was reaped from the victory.
An attempt was made on the following day to renew the
action and complete the enemy's destruction. But the
wind was gone. The light airs that prevailed were useless to the English ships, while they enabled the Dutch,
which were of shallower draught, to reach the refuge of
their own shoals and estuaries. However, the English
kept the sea, and a few days later were able to land on

the island of Schelling, sack the town of Brandaris, and
burn a fleet of one hundred and fifty merchantmen that
lay in the river.   By this one exploit damage to the
extent of over a million was done to the Dutch, and the
Duke was applauded once more to the echo by his
exulting country.   All August he cruised in the Channel,
making prizes, cutting out merchantmen, and preventing
a junction between the French and the Dutch; nor did
he return till just in time to receive the King's anxious
suggestion that he should come to London to allay the
panic which the great fire had created.   He was left
free to come or not as he liked, and much against his
will he came to his master's side.   The effect of his
presence was immediate, and Lord Arlington considered
that by his prompt return he had given the King his
throne a second time.

Disgusted as Monk was with the whole war and its
indecisive actions; with the weather that always interposed just as he was going to crush his despised foes;
with his young gentleman captains who only played at
fighting, and knew nothing of the sea but its slang;
with the old Commonwealth officers that would not do
their duty against the great Protestant Republic, there
was yet worse in store for the old patriot.

An empty treasury suggested a change of front
for the next year's campaign.   The Dutch clearly
meant to bleed the King to death with indecisive
engagements.   In order to rapidly and inexpensively
bring the enemy to terms, it was moved in the Council
to put the country in a state of defence, lay up the line-
of-battle ships, and prey on the Dutch commerce with
privateer cruisers.   Charles was against the idea, and

he was strongly supported by Monk and three others. Negotiations for peace were on foot, and the old general had no notion of treating except sword in hand. But the majority prevailed. The naval ports were directed to be fortified and the dismantled ships protected by booms. The idea was well enough, and had it only been carried out the Dutch might speedily have been brought to their knees; but although twice in the depth of winter the King went in person to inspect the progress of the works for the defence of the Thames and Medway, next to nothing was done. Disorder, insolvency, and corruption paralysed every effort, and after insulting the Scotch coasts, De Ruyter on Sunday June 9th, 1667, suddenly appeared off the Thames and threatened London itself.

A perfect panic prevailed. The banks stopped payment, the beacons were fired, and once more every eye was turned on the Duke of Albemarle. He was hard at work preparing to meet a descent on the threatened counties. Two days before, on the first alarm, Lord Oxford had been sent off to mobilise the militia in Essex, and Lord Middleton to do the same in Kent, while a bridge of boats was being got ready about Tilbury that the horse of either county might be rapidly moved to the support of the other. With the river he had nothing to do. It was under the Duke of York and the Admiralty, and Pett, one of the commissioners, was in special charge of Chatham and the Medway. At daybreak, however, on Monday morning the Dutch were seen at anchor at the Nore. A little later they began to move up the river, and at noon the King sent for Monk.

P

In four hours he was on his way to Chatham with the Guards to save the fleet and dock-yard, and at his heels half the young bloods in London were trailing pikes. As a soldier the lord-general's name had never been so much as breathed upon, and in a burst of enthusiasm a rabble "of idle lords and gentlemen, with their pistols and fooleries," started to their feet to follow the pattern of soldiership, the old Captain-Lieutenant of " Vere's," their fathers' father-in-arms. By night he reached Gravesend. It was practically defence-less. The batteries were unarmed and unmanned, and he decided to halt the train of artillery that was following him at the weak point till further orders. There was time for little more. His rest was disturbed with the sound of a furious cannonade from the direction of Sheerness, and at daylight he hurried on to Chatham.

Here, thanks to Monk's perfect organisation and his officers' high capacity, Lord Middleton was able to report the mobilisation of Kent complete, and the Duke to write off a letter to the King full of cheery con-fidence as to the result of any attempt of the Dutch to land. But that was the end; the rest of the news was too desperate to tell. Sheerness had fallen, and practically nothing had been done for the defence of Chatham. There was no ammunition, not a gun was mounted, the dock-yard hands had not been paid for months, and in desperation nearly the whole of them had deserted. In the face of stringent orders, the finest ships in the navy were still lying out unprotected in the tideway; most of the officials were away busily transporting their effects in the boats that had been provided for the defence of the fleet, and Pett was

panic-stricken. The only obstacle to the enemy's attack
was a chain which had been stretched across the
river below Upnor, but not a gun had been planted
for its protection. There was not even a gun-boat ready
to prevent the Dutch removing it.

Monk instantly sent back to Gravesend to order
on the artillery, and then hurried to the chain to throw
up flanking batteries. It was soon discovered that there
were not enough tools for the working-parties. More
were sent for, and answer came that they could
not be delivered without proper requisitions. Stickler
as Monk was for orderly routine, he was no man to see
his country strangled with red tape. With a sufficient
force he marched to the stores, broke them open, and
seized everything he wanted.

His next care was to arm and man Upnor Castle
opposite Chatham ; and to gain time till the works were
complete he ordered ships to be sunk in the channels
below the chain. To Pett and the most skilful pilots the
work was committed, and Monk went to superintend the
progress of the batteries. Five ships were sunk, and then,
that no precaution might be omitted, Admiral Sir Edward
Spragg was ordered to sound the channels in person to
make sure they were blocked. By this time the tide was
making fast and the Dutch were advancing on the flow.
At the last moment Spragg returned to say he had found
a deep channel quite clear. It was too late to stop it.
Not a gun was yet in its place. In the extremity of the
danger the veteran's old Quixotic spirit was rekindled
and set every heart on fire. By the chain lay two guardships which had been stationed there for its protection,
together with the *Monmouth*, which had just been fitted

out to join the northern cruising squadron. Unable to
witness in inactivity the insult which his old despised
enemies were about to put on his country, he determined
to man them with his troops. In person he went on board
the cruiser, resolved to die in defence of his old flagship
the *Royal Charles*, which lay a little above helpless and
dismantled, or at least determined not to survive his
country's disgrace. And with him went down into
the mouth of death fifty of the flower of England's dis-
solute Court, transformed for an hour to heroes by the
magic of the one stout old heart which knew not how
to flinch.

It would have been a worthy end could he and England's honour have fallen side by side. But it was not
to be. The newly discovered channel had not been
betrayed. The Dutch could not find it, and ere they had
cleared a way through the sunken ships the tide was
spent. A respite was won, but no rest. Sleepless and
untiring the lord-general worked on. Two ships were
placed in readiness to sink within the chain, and a large
Dutch prize was ordered to block the fair-way between
them. Pett was told to get the *Royal Charles* above the
dock by the evening tide, and Monk devoted himself to
the batteries.

On Wednesday at break of day he was still hard at
work. The redoubts were well forward, but the *Royal
Charles* had not been moved. The big Dutch prize was
being worked to its place, but it was only to be clumsily
stranded on a shoal, and in spite of all Monk's efforts
there was still nothing but the chain to protect the hulks
and the dock-yard as the tide turned.

At ten the Dutch, having cleared the channel in the

night, came boldly on with tide and wind, and after a hard struggle seized the guardships that Monk had manned. It was a moment of fearful anxiety as they prepared to charge the boom. A fire-ship led the way. It stuck on the top of it. A larger one followed, and with a crash the chain gave way. Then through the very channel that the Dutch prize should have blocked the enemy came on. In a few minutes two more guardships were on fire, and the grand old *Naseby* which had been launched twelve years ago, "with Oliver on horseback in the prow trampling six nations under foot;" which with changed name had proudly borne the King from exile to a throne; which not a year ago had wrung from Europe a cry of admiration while Monk's own flag was floating in tatters at its masthead,—was a prize in the hands of the Dutch.

"This was all I observed of the enemies' action on Wednesday," wrote the broken-hearted general with pathetic brevity when he reported to Parliament. He turned away—but not to grieve. Resistance and revenge were still his only thoughts. The other three great first-rates he sunk at their moorings, and then the artillery arrived. On the ebb the Dutch fell back with their prize, and all that day and the next morning the work of defence went on. "Courage mounted with occasion." Monk's spirit was upon them, and the fine lords and gentlemen toiled like cattle. They strained at the drag-ropes, they staggered under burdens, and when the hour was come they took their stand with ladle and linstock to work the guns.

When on Thursday at noon the Dutch came on once more fifty guns, besides those which had arrived from

Gravesend, were in position, and a furious fire was opened
on them. The Dutch stood on in spite of it, and engaged
Upnor Castle and the batteries with the coolest effrontery.
Between the broadsides English deserters on board the
enemy were heard jeering at the Government that had
cheated them of their pay, and under cover of the intrepid
attack the fire-ships passed on to where the three great
ships were sunk. They were still an easy prey. Their
upper works still towered above the water. Not a boat
was to be found to stop the progress of the fire-ships.
Helpless but defiant still, the old terror of the Dutch drew
down to the shore, and taking his stand, cane in hand,
with his Guards at his back, where the fire was hottest,
watched the humbling of the flag which he and Blake
and Oliver had raised so high. The fire-ships had
soon done their work : the three finest ships that were
left to England were a mass of flames ; and no ball had
come to end the bitterness of the old general's shame.

The Dutch retired with the ebb, and Monk, whom
since the morning the anxious King had been summoning
to his side to allay the panic in the capital, went up to
town. He had saved the dock-yard and two-thirds of
the fleet, but it did little to soothe his indignation, and
he reached Whitehall at two o'clock next morning
storming at those who had rejected his advice to fit out
the fleet and treat sword in hand. On his arrival a report
was circulated that he had been made Lord High Constable, and the immediate effect seems to have been a
restoration of confidence. Something like order and definite purpose was infused into the work of blocking the
Thames, and the Dutch thought fit to try and surprise
other ports. But everywhere they found to their cost that

they had no longer the Board of Admiralty to deal with. The hand of the lord-general was at every point, and wherever they attempted to land they were at once repulsed with loss. They returned to the Nore, but it was only to find that their old enemy had now set his mark there also. Thames and Medway bristled with guns and defensive works, and no further offensive operation was attempted till peace was signed.

Whatever was the fact, the country believed that old George had saved it from invasion and the miseries to which it had been exposed by Charles's treacherous councillors. The *Monmouth* incident was sung in ballads, and the general was compared to his immortal kinsman the great Sir Richard Grenville. Parliament met in a rage. Ravenous for a scapegoat, they went into committee on the late miscarriages, and the first result was a vote of thanks to the lord-general.

It was but little consolation to the old man. The disgrace at Chatham had been a terrible blow to him, and his tremendous exertions had told upon his shattered constitution. In despair he saw Charles return to the lap of his mistresses, indolent and profligate and careless as ever; and he fell back into the lethargy from which he had roused himself at his country's call. For some time it had been growing on him as his terrible disease advanced with secret strides. The following year dropsy declared itself, but still he clung to his post and occupied himself incessantly with the duties of his office. In the autumn, however, it became so bad, and was so complicated by an affection of the heart and lungs, that he was compelled to retire to Newhall, his seat in Essex, for rest and change of air. The old rumour that he had been

poisoned was revived, and caused great anger among the
people ;[1] for in him shone the only ray of hope, the only
spark of honesty amidst the night of treachery and corruption in which the country seemed lost.

During the winter he grew worse, but still neglected
all precautions. His extraordinary constitution had bred
in him a contempt for medicine and an insuperable impatience of the restraints which medical treatment en-
tailed. At last, however, being almost unable to breathe,
he was induced to try some pills invented by an old
soldier of his who had set up as a doctor. Strangely
enough he experienced immediate relief, and by the end
of the summer he returned to Whitehall thinking himself entirely cured. Once more he threw himself into
the business of State with something of his old ardour,
till with winter came a relapse to warn men that his end
was near.

Every one flocked to the Cockpit to pay his respects
to the renowned invalid and to look once more upon the
embodiment of the iron age that was past. Parliament
was sitting, and the great strife between the Houses over
Skinner's case was at its height. Lords and Commons
called on their way from Westminster, and forgetful even
then of all but his country's peace, the stout old general,
as he sat up in his chair wearily gasping for breath, implored them to come to a good understanding. Sir John
Grenville, now Earl of Bath, was assiduous in his attendance, and Gilbert Sheldon, the aged Archbishop of Canterbury, who all through the plague had stood unflinching
by the general's side, prayed with him constantly. Even
the laughter-loving King tore himself almost daily from

[1] Cf. Watts to Williamson, *S. P. Dom. Cal.*, July 17th, 1667.

the society of Lady Castlemaine to endure for a little while the distressing sight.

Though to the last Monk could not quite believe that his disease had mastered him, yet he viewed the prospect of his approaching death with the same quiet resolution with which he had looked it in the face a hundred times before.   He thought he still might live to staunch the bleeding wounds of his country and see its King a man again.   But if he might not raise it, he at least could leave it with little regret now it was sunk so low.   For years his own life had been a pattern of temperance and chastity, and the unblushing sin with which his great achievement had deluged the country was the source of real and poignant grief to him.

But one desire really bound him to life, and that was to see his son married.   Christopher was now a gallant of about eighteen years old, and ever since his father was first taken ill a marriage had been in course of arrangement between him and Lady Elizabeth Cavendish, granddaughter of the Duke of Newcastle.   Now at the eleventh hour the business was completed, and on December 30th the young couple were brought to the general's chamber.   There beside his chair, as he sat gasping for life, they were married, and the last faint effort of the arms that had lifted a king on to his throne was to take the silly girl he had chosen and place her feebly in the arms of the beloved son she was destined to ruin. It was a tragic wedding indeed, and with it the doom of the ancient house of Monk was sealed.   No child blessed the ill-omened union, and the extravagance of the half-witted bride soon drove the young duke to those evil courses which dragged him to his untimely end.   The last

of his race, he brought his father's name and titles in dis-
honour to the ground. With the crown of the Stuarts
fell the coronet of Albemarle. For by strange irony, as
William of Orange was on the eve of sailing to dethrone
the dynasty which the first duke had so triumphantly
restored, the last duke was dying in Jamaica a broken
gambler and a sot.

Happily ignorant of what he did, the dying father
resigned himself to the end which was now inevitable.
At four o'clock on New Year's morning, 1670, he insisted
on being removed to his sitting-room. Just ten years
ago in the fulness of his strength he had risen from
his uneasy couch at Coldstream to order his vanguard
to cross the Tweed on their eventful march. Now
as then, it was freezing bitterly, and no fire was alight.
Gumble hurried to his side. He saw death in the smile
which greeted him, and hastened to read the service for
the Visitation of the Sick. Later in the day the Sacra-
ment was administered, and the world knew the great
man was in extremity. All Sunday they flocked to take
their leave of him in such numbers that it was impossible
to keep the room clear for a minute. It was the
anniversary of the great day of his life, the Second of
January, when he himself at the head of his army had
crossed the Rubicon of the English Revolution, and like
Cromwell's, his victories seemed to cluster round his
head even as Death laid his hand upon it.

All night he lingered clinging to life. Erect in his
chair, as the people loved to remember, he defied even
Death to make him bend, and at the last received him
sitting like a king. To the end he maintained that he
would live if only the bitter frost would loose its grip,

and till dawn he obstinately held his enemy at bay. Then as the sun rose warm and bright and the frost began to break, the faithful Coldstreamers, who were watching in the silent chamber, heard "a single small groan," and the brave spirit of their chief was free at last.

With his George and Garter they hurried to the King. He received the news with genuine feeling as one that had lost a father. All that he owed to the stout heart that was still seemed to rush upon him like a loud warning from Heaven, and for a moment to rouse the magnanimity in which Monk had always believed. As though he could never reward enough the ungrudging service of his most faithful subject, he immediately despatched his Garter to Christopher, and announced that he should personally arrange the funeral. It was conducted in almost royal magnificence. After lying in state for some weeks in his armour as Captain-General, with his golden truncheon in his hand, his body was escorted to Westminster by the King in person in the midst of a procession which for splendour had only been rivalled at his own coronation, and there in Henry the Seventh's chapel it was laid with the bones of kings. And that no touch might be omitted to mark the exalted pedestal the majestic figure should occupy, the humblest of the great ones who were permitted to grace his last parade was the man on whom his cloak was to fall, the greatest of English generals, Ensign John Churchill.[1]

But there it all ended. No monument rose to mark the spot where the hero lay. The King was too poor,

---

[1] *London Gazette*, April 30th, 1670, by which it also appears that the King intended to raise a magnificent memorial to him.

the new duke too profligate, and the homely duchess died with broken heart while her lord still lay in state. Nor have any been found since save distant kinsmen even to show posterity where he lies. Neither the splendid regiment he founded, nor the army he inspired, nor the country to whom at so slight a cost he restored the priceless boon of monarchy, have thought him worthy of the tribute that has been lavished on so many not more deserving. So the memory of the man the King delighted to honour has fallen a victim to the execration of the visionaries he crushed, to the reproaches of the Puritans he restrained, to the rancour of the unjust stewards he exposed, to the abjectness of the servile historiographers with whom half his career was a subject tabooed, and to the jibes of the profligates with whom he would not sin.

For a biographer to sum up a character so lovable and so misunderstood is almost impossible without falling into exaggeration. It is better that his story should close with a tribute dropped unwittingly from the most unwilling hand that could have penned it. On October 24th, 1667, for the last time the House awarded the sturdy old patriot their thanks for his service; "Which is a strange act," wrote Pepys; "but, I know not how, the blockhead Albemarle hath strange luck to be loved, though he be (and every man must know it) the heaviest man in the world, but stout and honest to his country."

In the sermon that was delivered at his funeral in Westminster Abbey we have the opinion of a great dignitary of the Church who was fully alive to his faults. Careful as he was that he should pronounce no idle panegyric, he blessed him altogether. "He was the best father in the world," said the Bishop of Exeter. "He was certainly the best husband in the world, and he received the requital of faithfulness and love. They twain were loving in their lives and in death they were not divided. . . . He was the favourite of Parliament, the darling of the Houses. They confided in him. They loved and revered him." And of the King's affection he had as high a testimony to give.

Such abiding popularity as his is a thing not lightly won. It is not for long that a great nation will honour a man unworthy of its devotion. Through ten years of doubt and danger and shifting party-strife he was the idol of the people of England, and if it is asked why we should endorse the verdict of his contemporaries, the answer is plain; he wound up the English Revolution. At the high tide of profit he struck a balance and closed the account. Elsewhere, under stars less fortunate than our own, no liquidator has arisen to do the work which only a man of Monk's inflexible integrity and splendid self-control can accomplish, and there we have seen Revolution drag on a bankrupt existence with ever accumulating loss. From that Monk saved us. It was what Cromwell strove to do and failed, for the hour was not yet ripe. With an exactness which it is impossible to account for or ignore Monk marked the hour when it came, gripped it with confident decision, and the fate of the sovereign who tried to set at nought the English Revolution proves the dull soldier was right.

Printed by R. & R. CLARK, *Edinburgh.*